THE FINANCIAL WAR ON TERRORISM

A guide

by the Financial Action Task Force

The Financial Action Task Force was established in 1989 at the Paris Summit of leaders of the Group of Seven Nations and the President of the European Commission. Its brief was to co-ordinate and spearhead an international campaign against criminal money laundering. After the September 11 attacks on the United States, its responsibilities were widened in October 2001 to include the fight against the financing of terrorism.

The FATF is an independent international body whose Secretariat is housed at the Paris headquarters of the Organisation for Economic Co-operation and Development.

The thirty-one member countries and governments of the FATF are: Argentina; Australia, Austria; Belgium; Brazil; Canada; Denmark; Finland; France; Germany; Greece; Hong Kong, China; Iceland; Ireland; Italy; Japan; Luxembourg; Mexico; the Kingdom of the Netherlands; New Zealand; Norway; Portugal; the Russian Federation; Singapore; South Africa; Spain; Sweden; Switzerland; Turkey; United Kingdom; and the United States. The European Commission and the Gulf Co-operation Council are also members of the FATF, while five FATF-style regional bodies and more than 15 other international organisations or bodies have observer status. A list of all members and observers can be found on the FATF website at *http://www.fatf-gafi.org/Members_en.htm*.

All rights reserved.
Applications for permission to reproduce all
or part of this publication should be made to:
FATF Secretariat,
2 rue André Pascal,
75775 Paris Cedex 16, France

Fax: 33 (0)1 45 24 17 60
e-mail: contact@fatf-gafi.org

Contents

Preface . . . . p. 5

Introduction . . . . p. 7

Executive Summary . . . . p. 12

PART 1: TERRORIST FINANCING

The FATF Eight Special Recommendations . . . . p. 18

Interpretative Notes and Best Practices

    Special Recommendation III: Freezing and Confiscating
Terrorist Assets . . . . p. 23

    Special Recommendation VI: Alternative Remittance . . . . p. 41

    Special Recommendation VII: Wire Transfers . . . . p. 57

    Special Recommendation VIII: Non-Profit Organisations . . . . . p. 61

Guidance for Financial Institutions in Detecting
Terrorist Financing . . . . p. 71

PART 2: MONEY LAUNDERING

The FATF Forty Recommendations . . . . p. 91

Glossary . . . . p. 111

Interpretative Notes . . . . p. 115

ANNEX

Respondents to the FATF Self Assessment Exercise for the
Eight Special Recommendations on Terrorist Financing . . . . p. 125

PREFACE

By FATF XIV President Jochen Sanio

In October 2001, the Financial Action Task Force (FATF) adopted the Eight Special Recommendations on Terrorist Financing which set out the key legislative and regulatory steps that countries need to put in place to stop the financing of terrorism. Since then, the FATF has become the world's most important standard setter in the fight against terrorist financing, and has worked to promote international awareness and co-operation in this regard.

For the German Presidency of FATF XIV countering the financing of terrorism has been a top priority. Only the commitment of the broad international community to fight terrorist financing and close global co-operation on the basis of internationally agreed standards will help us to succeed in our fight against these threats. Accordingly, FATF XIV has called on all countries around the world, both members and non-members alike, to join in the FATF's efforts by taking comprehensive steps to dry up the flow of funds to terrorists.

Terrorist financing, like money laundering and corruption, is accomplished through various techniques which abuse financial markets. Safeguarding the transparency of money flows of both formal and informal sector values transfers is a key element in disrupting both money laundering and terrorist financing. Protecting the world's financial systems by effectively implementing international standards to combat terrorist financing and money laundering techniques remains the FATF's highest priority.

Consequently, the cornerstone of the FATF's anti-money laundering (AML)/counter-terrorist financing (CFT) strategy is to increase the transparency and oversight of payments and payment systems and to encourage the detection and vigorous prosecution of illegal financial transactions which occur outside of the regulated financial sector. It is only the terrorist, the money launderer and the people behind them who profit from opaque financial structures and who gain from lax regulation in this field. Indeed, improving the transparency of the financial system and financial flows through the formal financial sector is the most effective strategic instrument with which to respond to both money laundering and terrorist financing.

Since the adoption of the Eight Special Recommendations, the international community has made significant progress in the fight against this social and economic evil. The United Nations Security Council Resolutions have led to the freezing of more than 138 million US Dollars. This, in turn, has restricted the scope for abusing the financial system to finance terrorism.

Uniform implementation of the Recommendations will be ensured by mutual evaluations of member governments to be carried out by the FATF. No less important is the close co-operation between the FATF, the IMF, and the World Bank concerning AML/CFT assessments. This co-operation, which was agreed to in FATF XIV, has evolved well in a short space of time. In addition to these new forms of co-operation with the IMF and World Bank, the FATF will continue its efforts to co-operate with other international organisations in the area of AML/CFT. This will also help to anchor the FATF standards on terrorist financing on a global scale.

In passing the Eight Special Recommendations in October 2001, the FATF has created a robust standard against terrorist financing which ensures the transparency of financial flows. The Eight Special Recommendations are complementary to the FATF Forty Recommendations which were revised in June 2003. Together the Eight Special Recommendations and the revised Forty Recommendations constitute a new comprehensive framework for combating money laundering and terrorist financing.

I am sure that the implementation of all the FATF standards and the intensive international co-operation against terrorist financing will prove to be effective. The aim of this book is to make a significant contribution to this process and to guide countries in the financial war on terrorism.

Jochen Sanio
President of the Federal Financial Supervisory Authority (Bonn),
Federal Republic of Germany
President of FATF XIV

Bonn, 2004

INTRODUCTION

Terrorism destroys by fear. Terrorists maim and kill; but they also attack society in deeper ways. Like a virus, terrorism penetrates and colonises healthy economic and social bodies, propagating itself while destroying them.

It prospers by destroying trust, which is the underlying requirement for civil order.

The business of terrorism is destruction. At the same time, terrorism is a business – a deadly, corrosive and criminal business – and, like all businesses, terrorism requires money. In recognition of this fact, the international community has turned its attention to preventing the financing of terrorism, terrorist acts and terrorist organisations.

Whatever its religious, political or ideological pretensions, terrorism operates through business mechanisms. Its agents are paid; their weapons are purchased; their plots are financed; their organisations raise, transfer, invest and spend hundreds of millions of dollars every year.

Good governments have a common interest in protecting the civil order that terrorism destroy. Police and intelligence services are their front-line defence. But behind the front-line, a long-term strategic blockade is fighting terrorist organisations by identifying and freezing the financial assets and flows that are their lifeblood.

The Financial Action Task Force is the international co-ordinator of this financial war, mandated after September 11 to oversee the hunt for terrorist money because of its track record fostering global co-operation against criminal money laundering. The fight to freeze terrorist financing is immediate and urgent and experience shows that international criminal and terrorist financing channels are often the same.

The FATF harnesses to a common cause the energy and resources of its 33 members, all of which work together in an extensive world-wide network of collaborating governments, regional and international organisations and bodies. This book is intended for all those who want to sign up to that cause, offering practical guidance on what to do, and how to do it.

The Financial War on Terrorism brings together the key recommendations, guidelines and operational templates painstakingly developed and honed by FATF working groups over more than a decade. It sets out a step-by-step illustrated roadmap for those whose job it is to put in place and enforce mutually consistent laws, mechanisms and collaborative processes to choke the flow of funds to terrorist organisations.

Terrorist funding, like criminal money laundering, disguises itself as legitimate activity. Trading companies, banks, even charities may all be subverted. Financial institutions and regulators need to be constantly alert to the telltale signs that point to a secret agenda. *The Financial War on Terrorism* offers concrete illustrations of the ways that terrorists hide their business dealings, and the ways that financial institutions, regulators and law enforcement agencies need to work together to root them out.

Investigators in FATF member countries have identified the common tricks of the terrorist financial trade. Dummy companies are set up to house assets and run bank accounts; charities are used with or without their knowledge and consent, to collect, transfer and pay out money. Terrorist funds are mixed into businesses (which may or may not be otherwise legitimate) and shipped from country to country using wire transfers, underground moneychangers and black market operators.

In Spain, police have found front companies for the armed Basque independence movement ETA in businesses as diverse as printing and publishing, real estate, fisheries and entertainment. In one case a group of taverns in the Basque Country was found to have raised more than 30 million dollars for ETA through loans secured on their properties and other assets.

In Japan, an illegal money transfer circuit with suspected terrorist links was uncovered two months after September 11 in a car parts business trading with Pakistan.

United States investigators, unravelling the financial networks behind the destruction of the World Trade Center, found delicatessens doubling as fund collection centres, million-dollar cash transfers disguised as honey shipments, multi-million transfers broken down into hundreds of small transactions of less than $10 00 dollars each to slip unnoticed through normal banking channels. Following up its investigations, the US took legal action to freeze nearly $10 million belonging to a dozen relief organisations that it claimed were being used to divert charitable donations to Al-Qaida, Hamas and other terrorist groups.

One of the problems facing governments in their battle with terrorism is the world-wide proliferation of informal, unlicensed money remittance schemes.

For the world's poor migrant workers, often driven from their homes by war and starvation, these offer a cheap and efficient way of sending money back to support the families they have had to leave behind. The trouble is that because they are informal and uncontrolled they also offer an open door to criminal and terrorist exploitation.

An example: out of more than a decade of tribal and civil war in Somalia several remittance structures emerged to serve the needs of an estimated 750 000 migrants and displaced refugees. Two in particular, Al Barakaat and Dahabshiil, provided a vital financial link for people too marginalised to have access to the global banking system: but in the wake of September 11, investigators in the United States identified Al Barakaat as a funding channel for Al-Qaida, successfully prosecuting three Barakaat officials for carrying out more than $10 million in illegal international fund transfers; and in Europe, investigators tracking Al-Qaida's German connections were led to a worldwide illegal banking network operating through Dahabshiil offices in, for example, Canada, Denmark, Germany, Italy, New Zealand, Saudi Arabia the United Kingdom and the United States.

One of the hardest and most sensitive challenges facing responsible governments is to work, separately and together, to block terrorist funds from transiting such informal channels without at the same time cutting off the world's dispossessed from the homes and families to which they hope one day to return.

As the focal point of international resistance to terrorism, the Financial Action Task Force has identified two basic operating principles. The first is the need to collaborate with the United Nations. This means respecting, ratifying and implementing its anti-terrorist treaties and resolutions.

The second is the need for legislators to identify, define and criminalise terrorist financial activity; and to set in place fair and effective mechanisms to freeze, seize, and ultimately confiscate terrorist assets.

This is not easy, and cannot be done by governments in isolation. Internationally, it calls for co-operation that must combine openness with sensitivity to national sovereignty and security concerns; nationally, it calls for co-operation between public and private sectors that both recognises common interest and protects legitimate confidentiality.

On the international front the starting point for all governments and legislators must be the ratification and implementation of the 1999 UN Convention for the Suppression of the Financing of Terrorism.

On the domestic front, the starting point must be the adoption of clear, detailed and precise laws that specifically criminalise the financing of terrorism and related money-laundering activities.

With the national and international legal framework in place, the next step is to establish prompt and effective regulatory and administrative mechanisms for identifying, freezing and (if justified by legal process) confiscating suspected terrorist assets. These mechanisms must, at a minimum, enable national governments and their agents to respond to the multiple UN Security Council resolutions adopted since 1999 to ensure co-ordinated international action against identified terrorist groups and their associates. Beyond that, they need to encourage and facilitate the reporting of suspicious transactions by banks and other financial institutions, and the freest possible inter-governmental exchange of information and legal assistance.

These are relatively easy and uncontroversial things to do, in the sense that they involve dealing with people and organisations that are used to working within the normal regulatory relationships of the formal economy. But the formal economy is only part of the picture. Unless regulatory authorities can also interface with the informal economy, terrorist funds barred from the global banking system will continue to flow through invisible parallel channels. This is why it is essential to establish visibility and traceability requirements for all money-collection and transfer activities, including those of the informal economy and the non-profit charity sector.

For cultural and political reasons this may be hard to achieve. Informal money transfer organisations often serve migrant or minority communities, which may be alienated from mainstream society; charities may have priorities that conflict with those of government.

To achieve transparency in the informal and non-profit sectors of the economy, regulation, supervision and enforcement are not enough. These are instruments for the prevention of terrorism; but they will not work without co-operation, which calls for trust. Alongside measures for the identification, freezing and seizing of terrorist assets there must be confidence-building measures to protect legitimate confidentiality and property rights.

In these sensitive and delicate areas as well as in the more conventional spheres of legislation and enforcement, the Financial Action Task Force and its members offer guidance and example to all jurisdictions that seek to join in the financial war against terrorism. As the terrorist threat evolves, so too must the counter-terrorist response; part of the process therefore is a constant and self-critical re-appraisal of the adequacy of national and international counter-terrorist regimes.

In October 2001 the FATF started a self-assessment programme to monitor the progress of its campaign to outlaw the business of terror.

By 2003 more than 130 countries and territories, ranging in size from Russia and China to Macau and San Marino had taken a first step forward by filing responses to the FATF's self-assessment questionnaire, distributed globally via the FATF website at *http://www.fatf-gafi.org/pdf/SAQTF03_en.doc* in English, and *http://www.fatf-gafi.org/pdf/SAQTF03_fr.doc* in French.

The FATF hopes that by bringing together its recommendations, explanatory texts and best practice guidelines in one easily accessible volume it will encourage a new and wider audience to join the campaign against one of the most pernicious evils of our times.

Executive Summary

The Financial War on Terrorism combines in one volume the eight special counter-terrorist recommendations of the Financial Action Task Force with the FATF's 40 underlying recommendations for combating money laundering and a series of explanatory notes and practical guidelines. The book offers co-operating governments, legislators, regulators and financial institutions practical help in designing and implementing financial regimes to halt the flow of funding to terrorists and their organisations. An annex lists jurisdictions which, at date of publication, have co-operated by responding to an FATF self-assessment questionnaire.

Part 1. *The FATF Special Recommendations on Terrorist Financing, with Interpretative Notes and Best Practice Papers.*

The FATF's Special Recommendations on Terrorist Financing, combined with its 40 Recommendations on money laundering, set out the basic framework for detecting, preventing and suppressing the financing of terrorism and terrorist acts.

The Eight Special Recommendations propose that all countries should:

- Immediately ratify and implement the 1999 United Nations Convention for the Suppression of the Financing of Terrorism, and implement related UN Security Council resolutions.
- Criminalize terrorist financing and ensure that any proceeds from terrorist crimes are subject to anti-money laundering measures.
- Implement all necessary measures for suspected funds and property of terrorists, those who finance them and terrorist organisations to be frozen without delay, seized and, if subsequently justified, confiscated.
- Require banks and other businesses subject to anti-money laundering obligations to report suspected terrorist-linked funds to the competent authorities.
- Adopt treaties or other mutual aid mechanisms providing maximum possible legal assistance and information to foreign jurisdictions conducting investigations, prosecutions and enforcement proceedings related to terrorist financing.
- Put in place all possible measures including, where possible, extradition procedures, to avoid being used as safe havens by individuals charged with terrorist financing offences.
- License or register all operators of money transmission services, formal or informal, and subject them to the FATF Recommendations that apply to banks and other financial institutions, with appropriate penalties for illegal operators.

- Require financial institutions, including remittance operators, to accompany fund transfers and related messages with accurate and meaningful originator information that stays with the transfer or message through the payment chain.

- Act to ensure that financial institutions take steps to detect fund transfers that lack complete originator information and to report such transfers if they are suspicious.

- Review and if necessary tighten the legal and regulatory framework for non-profit organisations and other vulnerable entities to ensure that they cannot be abused or misused for terrorist financing purposes.

The FATF's interpretative notes and best practice papers focus on four of the eight special counter-terrorist recommendations:

- SR III on the freezing, seizing and confiscation of the funds and assets of terrorists, those who finance terrorism and terrorist organisations.

- SR VI on increasing the transparency and accountability of alternative remittance systems.

- SR VII on increasing the transparency and counter-terrorist scrutiny of wire transfers.

- SR VIII on combating the terrorist abuse of non-profit organisations.

In particular, the Interpretative Note for SR III highlights four obligations. The first requires jurisdictions to put in place mechanisms enabling them to freeze identified terrorist-related funds and assets without delay, in accordance with specific United Nations resolutions concerning Al-Qaida, the Taliban, asssociated individuals and other persons or organisations designated by the United Nations Security Council. The second requires jurisdictions to put in place mechanisms enabling them to freeze terrorist-related funds and assets without delay, in accordance with United Nations resolutions 1373 (2001) concerning persons or organisations designated by individual countries. The third requires jurisdictions to put in place mechanisms enabling them to freeze or, where appropriate, seize terrorist-related funds and assets that have been identified as being related to terrorism, but which have not been designated under any United Nations resolutions. The fourth requires jurisdictions to put in place confiscation mechanisms based on due process.

The Best Practice Paper, based on experience, offers a benchmark for developing the institutional, legal and procedural structures of an effective terrorist finance freezing regime.

The Interpretative Note and Best Practice Paper for SR VI aim to increase the transparency of payment flows through informal alternative remittance systems.

The Interpretative Note highlights three core requirements: the licensing or registration of all money transfer service providers, including those in the informal sector; the application of all FATF recommendations to all transfer services; and the application of sanctions against unlicensed and non-compliant service providers.

The Best Practice Paper focuses on practical suggestions for identifying and licensing or registering informal transfer services, and ensuring that they put in place proper accounts, with customer identification, record keeping and suspicious transaction reporting procedures.

The Interpretative Note for SR VII lays out a framework for preventing terrorists and other criminals from moving funds by domestic or international wire transfer (that is, electronic transfer between financial institutions) and detecting such movements if they occur. Specifically it aims to ensure that basic originator information is available to law enforcement and financial intelligence authorities, and to the financial institutions that are responsible for reporting suspicious activity.

The Best Practice Paper for SR VIII highlights the abuse by terrorists and terrorist groups of non-profit organisations, which collect and disburse donations worth hundreds of billions of dollars a year. Charities and other non-profit organisations take many legal forms. The Best Practice Paper therefore favours a functional rather than a legalistic solution to the risk of abuse. The best practices call for flexible, light-handed government oversight of the non-profit sector, and close co-operation with the charitable community to promote self-regulation, transparency and accountability. The Best Practice Paper stresses the importance of effective auditing, adequate verification of charitable programmes, and the use, where possible, of the formal banking system to manage charity funds.

The Guidance Paper for Financial Institutions seeks to ensure that banks and other financial businesses do not unknowingly hide or move terrorist funds. It describes general and specific characteristics of terrorist financing and provides a series of case studies showing how law enforcement and financial intelligence authorities can use information from the financial institutions to identify and prosecute terrorist financial activity. It also offers detailed advice to financial institutions to help them identify the telltale signs that point to a need for heightened surveillance of potentially suspect transactions.

Annexes to the Guidance Paper for Financial Institutions describe the characteristics of transactions that may call for increased scrutiny, and list UN and other sources of relevant information.

Part 2. *The 40 Recommendations to combat Money Laundering and Terrorist Financing.*

The FATF's 40 Recommendations, revised and expanded in June 2003, set internationally-recognized standards for combating money laundering and, by extension, terrorist financing.

The Recommendations cover legal systems; measures to be taken by financial and other economic operators; institutional and other systemic requirements; and international co-operation.

- The first three recommendations set out a legal and systemic framework for defining the scope of the criminal offence of money laundering, and adopting measures to freeze, seize, and confiscate money laundering proceeds or instruments.

- Recommendations 4 – 25 propose requirements for transparency in the financial industry, including customer identification, on-going due diligence and record keeping by financial institutions, trustee service providers, accountants, lawyers and precious commodity dealers; suspicious transaction reporting requirements for those businesses and professions, with compliance programmes for financial institutions. Other deterrent measures including action to isolate and suppress shell banking; relationships involving countries that are non-compliant with FATF Recommendations; and the regulation and supervision of financial institutions and other targeted businesses or professions, including notably the gambling industry.

- Recommendations 26 – 34 deal with the institutional and other measures required to establish effective systems for combating money laundering and terrorist financing, including the designation of competent authorities and attribution of their powers and resources; and measures to enhance the transparency of asset ownership and control.

- Recommendations 35 – 40 deal with international co-operation, including ratification and implementation of relevant international agreements such as the Vienna and Palermo Conventions, the 1999 UN Convention for the Suppression of the Financing of Terrorism, the 1990 Council of Europe Convention on Laundering and the 2002 Inter-American Convention against Terrorism. The Recommendations cover mutual legal assistance and other forms of co-operation such as the opening of clear and effective gateways for information exchanges and mutual assistance in investigations. They also stipulate the requirement that countries should establish controls and safeguards to ensure the proper and limited use of exchanged information, with specific reference to privacy and data protection rights.

The 40 Recommendations are accompanied by a glossary defining the terminology used, and interpretatative notes to guide jurisdictions in their implementation.

A concluding annex lists the more than 130 countries and territories which by end-2003 had filed co-operative responses to the self-assessment questionnaire designed by the FATF to monitor compliance with its recommendations.

PART 1: TERRORIST FINANCING

The FATF Eight Special Recommendations   p. 18

Interpretative Notes and Best Practices

    Special Recommendation III: Freezing and Confiscating
    Terrorist Assets   p. 23

    Special Recommendation VI: Alternative Remittance   p. 41

    Special Recommendation VII: Wire Transfers   p. 57

    Special Recommendation VIII: Non-Profit Organisations   p. 61

Guidance for Financial Institutions in Detecting
Terrorist Financing   p. 71

THE FATF EIGHT SPECIAL RECOMMENDATIONS

Recognising the vital importance of taking action to combat the financing of terrorism, the FATF has agreed these Recommendations, which, when combined with the FATF Forty Recommendations on money laundering, set out the basic framework to detect, prevent and suppress the financing of terrorism and terrorist acts.

I. **Ratification and Implementation of UN Instruments**

Each country should take immediate steps to ratify and to implement fully the 1999 United Nations International Convention for the Suppression of the Financing of Terrorism. Countries should also immediately implement the United Nations resolutions relating to the prevention and suppression of the financing of terrorist acts, particularly United Nations Security Council Resolution 1373.

II. **Criminalising the financing of terrorism and associated money laundering**

Each country should criminalise the financing of terrorism, terrorist acts and terrorist organisations. Countries should ensure that such offences are designated as money laundering predicate offences.

III. **Freezing and confiscating terrorist assets**

Each country should implement measures to freeze without delay funds or other assets of terrorists, those who finance terrorism and terrorist organisations in accordance with the United Nations resolutions relating to the prevention and suppression of the financing of terrorist acts. Each country should also adopt and implement measures, including legislative ones, which would enable the competent authorities to seize and confiscate property that is the proceeds of, or used in, or intended or allocated for use in, the financing of terrorism, terrorist acts or terrorist organisations.

IV. **Reporting suspicious transactions related to terrorism**

If financial institutions, or other businesses or entities subject to anti-money laundering obligations, suspect or have reasonable grounds to suspect that funds are linked or related to, or are to be used for terrorism, terrorist acts or by terrorist organisations, they should be required to report promptly their suspicions to the competent authorities.

V. **International co-operation**

Each country should afford another country, on the basis of a treaty, arrangement or other mechanism for mutual legal assistance or information exchange, the greatest possible measure of assistance in connection with criminal, civil enforcement, and administrative investigations, inquiries and proceedings relating to the financing of terrorism, terrorist acts and terrorist organisations. Countries should also take all possible measures to ensure that they do not provide safe havens for individuals charged with the financing of terrorism, terrorist acts or terrorist organisations, and should have procedures in place to extradite, where possible, such individuals.

VI. Alternative remittance

Each country should take measures to ensure that persons or legal entities, including agents, that provide a service for the transmission of money or value, including transmission through an informal money or value transfer system or network, should be licensed or registered and subject to all the FATF Recommendations that apply to banks and non-bank financial institutions. Each country should ensure that persons or legal entities that carry out this service illegally are subject to administrative, civil or criminal sanctions.

VII. Wire transfers

Countries should take measures to require financial institutions, including money remitters, to include accurate and meaningful originator information (name, address and account number) on funds transfers and related messages that are sent, and the information should remain with the transfer or related message through the payment chain. Countries should take measures to ensure that financial institutions, including money remitters, conduct enhanced scrutiny of and monitor for suspicious activity funds transfers which do not contain complete originator information (name, address and account number).

VIII. Non-profit organisations

Countries should review the adequacy of laws and regulations that relate to entities that can be abused for the financing of terrorism. Non-profit organisations are particularly vulnerable, and countries should ensure that they cannot be misused:

   i) by terrorist organisations posing as legitimate entities;
   ii) to exploit legitimate entities as conduits for terrorist financing, including for the purpose of escaping asset freezing measures; and
   iii) to conceal or obscure the clandestine diversion of funds intended for legitimate purposes to terrorist organisations.

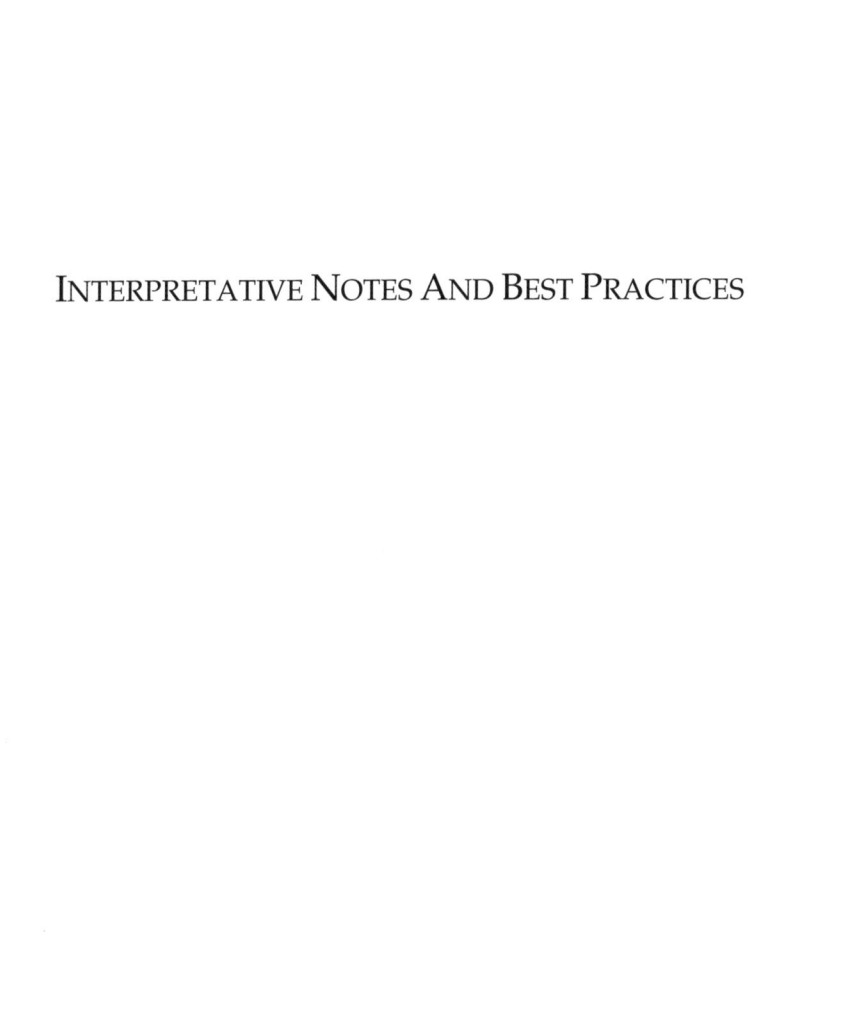

Interpretative Notes And Best Practices

SPECIAL RECOMMENDATION III: FREEZING AND CONFISCATING TERRORIST ASSETS

INTERPRETATIVE NOTE

Objectives

1. FATF Special Recommendation III consists of two obligations. The first requires jurisdictions to implement measures that will freeze or, if appropriate, seize terrorist-related funds or other assets without delay in accordance with relevant United Nations resolutions. The second obligation of Special Recommendation III is to have measures in place that permit a jurisdiction to seize or confiscate terrorist funds or other assets on the basis of an order or mechanism issued by a competent authority or a court.

2. The objective of the first requirement is to freeze terrorist-related funds or other assets based on reasonable grounds, or a reasonable basis, to suspect or believe that such funds or other assets could be used to finance terrorist activity. The objective of the second requirement is to deprive terrorists of these funds or other assets if and when links have been adequately established between the funds or other assets and terrorists or terrorist activity. The intent of the first objective is preventative, while the intent of the second objective is mainly preventative and punitive. Both requirements are necessary to deprive terrorists and terrorist networks of the means to conduct future terrorist activity and maintain their infrastructure and operations.

Scope

3. Special Recommendation III is intended, with regard to its first requirement, to complement the obligations in the context of the United Nations Security Council (UNSC) resolutions relating to the prevention and suppression of the financing of terrorist acts—S/RES/1267(1999) and its successor resolutions,[1] S/RES/1373(2001) and any prospective resolutions related to the

---

[1] When issued, S/RES/1267(1999) had a time limit of one year. A series of resolutions have been issued by the United Nations Security Council (UNSC) to extend and further refine provisions of S/RES/1267(1999). By successor resolutions are meant those resolutions that

freezing, or if appropriate seizure, of terrorist assets. It should be stressed that none of the obligations in Special Recommendation III is intended to replace other measures or obligations that may already be in place for dealing with funds or other assets in the context of a criminal, civil or administrative investigation or proceeding.[2] The focus of Special Recommendation III instead is on the preventative measures that are necessary and unique in the context of stopping the flow or use of funds or other assets to terrorist groups.

4. S/RES/1267(1999) and S/RES/1373(2001) differ in the persons and entities whose funds or other assets are to be frozen, the authorities responsible for making these designations, and the effect of these designations.

5. S/RES/1267(1999) and its successor resolutions obligate jurisdictions to freeze without delay the funds or other assets owned or controlled by Al-Qaida, the Taliban, Usama bin Laden, or persons and entities associated with them as designated by the United Nations Al-Qaida and Taliban Sanctions Committee established pursuant to United Nations Security Council Resolution 1267 (the Al-Qaida and Taliban Sanctions Committee), including funds derived from funds or other assets owned or controlled, directly or indirectly, by them or by persons acting on their behalf or at their direction, and ensure that neither these nor any other funds or other assets are made available, directly or indirectly, for such persons' benefit, by their nationals or by any person within their territory. The Al-Qaida and Taliban Sanctions Committee is the authority responsible for designating the persons and entities that should have their funds or other assets frozen under S/RES/1267(1999). All jurisdictions that are members of the United Nations are obligated by S/RES/1267(1999) to freeze the assets of persons and entities so designated by the Al-Qaida and Taliban Sanctions Committee.[3]

---

extend and are directly related to the original resolution S/RES/1267(1999). At the time of issue of this Interpretative Note, these resolutions included S/RES/1333(2000), S/RES/1363(2001), S/RES/1390(2002) and S/RES/1455(2003). In this Interpretative Note, the term S/RES/1267(1999) refers to S/RES/1267(1999) and its successor resolutions.

[2] For instance, both the UN Convention against Illicit Traffic in Narcotic Drugs and Psychotropic Substances (1988) and UN Convention against Transnational Organised Crime (2000) contain obligations regarding freezing, seizure and confiscation in the context of combating transnational crime. Those obligations exist separately and apart from obligations that are set forth in S/RES/1267(1999), S/RES/1373(2001) and Special Recommendation III.

[3] When the UNSC acts under Chapter VII of the UN Charter, the resolutions it issues are mandatory for all UN members.

6. S/RES/1373(2001) obligates jurisdictions[4] to freeze without delay the funds or other assets of persons who commit, or attempt to commit, terrorist acts or participate in or facilitate the commission of terrorist acts; of entities owned or controlled directly or indirectly by such persons; and of persons and entities acting on behalf of, or at the direction of such persons and entities, including funds or other assets derived or generated from property owned or controlled, directly or indirectly, by such persons and associated persons and entities. Each individual jurisdiction has the authority to designate the persons and entities that should have their funds or other assets frozen. Additionally, to ensure that effective co-operation is developed among jurisdictions, jurisdictions should examine and give effect to, if appropriate, the actions initiated under the freezing mechanisms of other jurisdictions. When *i)* a specific notification or communication is sent and *ii)* the jurisdiction receiving the request is satisfied, according to applicable legal principles, that a requested designation is supported by reasonable grounds, or a reasonable basis, to suspect or believe that the proposed designee is a terrorist, one who finances terrorism or a terrorist organisation, the jurisdiction receiving the request must ensure that the funds or other assets of the designated person are frozen without delay.

Definitions

7. For the purposes of Special Recommendation III and this Interpretative Note, the following definitions apply:

a) The term *freeze* means to prohibit the transfer, conversion, disposition or movement of funds or other assets on the basis of, and for the duration of the validity of, an action initiated by a competent authority or a court under a freezing mechanism. The frozen funds or other assets remain the property of the person(s) or entity(ies) that held an interest in the specified funds or other assets at the time of the freezing and may continue to be administered by the financial institution or other arrangements designated by such person(s) or entity(ies) prior to the initiation of an action under a freezing mechanism.

b) The term *seize* means to prohibit the transfer, conversion, disposition or movement of funds or other assets on the basis of an action initiated by a competent authority or a court under a freezing mechanism. However, unlike a freezing action, a seizure is effected by a mechanism that allows the competent authority or court to take control of specified funds or other assets. The seized funds or other assets remain the property of the person(s) or entity(ies) that held an interest in the specified funds or other assets at the time of the seizure, although the competent authority or court will often take over possession, administration or management of the seized funds or other assets.

---

[4] The UNSC was acting under Chapter VII of the UN Charter in issuing S/RES/1373(2001) (see previous footnote).

c) The term *confiscate*, which includes forfeiture where applicable, means the permanent deprivation of funds or other assets by order of a competent authority or a court. Confiscation or forfeiture takes place through a judicial or administrative procedure that transfers the ownership of specified funds or other assets to be transferred to the State. In this case, the person(s) or entity(ies) that held an interest in the specified funds or other assets at the time of the confiscation or forfeiture loses all rights, in principle, to the confiscated or forfeited funds or other assets.[5]

d) The term *funds or other assets* means financial assets, property of every kind, whether tangible or intangible, movable or immovable, however acquired, and legal documents or instruments in any form, including electronic or digital, evidencing title to, or interest in, such funds or other assets, including, but not limited to, bank credits, travellers cheques, bank cheques, money orders, shares, securities, bonds, drafts, or letters of credit, and any interest, dividends or other income on or value accruing from or generated by such funds or other assets.

e) The term *terrorist* refers to any natural person who: *i)* commits, or attempts to commit, terrorist acts[6] by any means, directly or indirectly, unlawfully and wilfully; *ii)* participates as an accomplice in terrorist acts or terrorist financing; *iii)* organises or directs others to commit terrorist acts or terrorist financing; or *iv)* contributes to the commission of terrorist acts or terrorist financing by a group of persons acting with a common purpose where the contribution is made intentionally and with the aim of furthering the terrorist act or terrorist financing or with the knowledge of the intention of the group to commit a terrorist act or terrorist financing.

---

[5] Confiscation or forfeiture orders are usually linked to a criminal conviction or a court decision whereby the confiscated or forfeited property is determined to have been derived from or intended for use in a violation of the law.

[6] A terrorist act includes an act which constitutes an offence within the scope of, and as defined in one of the following treaties: Convention for the Suppression of Unlawful Seizure of Aircraft, Convention for the Suppression of Unlawful Acts against the Safety of Civil Aviation, Convention on the Prevention and Punishment of Crimes against Internationally Protected Persons, including Diplomatic Agents, International Convention against the Taking of Hostages, Convention on the Physical Protection of Nuclear Material, Protocol for the Suppression of Unlawful Acts of Violence at Airports Serving International Civil Aviation, supplementary to the Convention for the Suppression of Unlawful Acts against the Safety of Civil Aviation, Convention for the Suppression of Unlawful Acts against the Safety of Maritime Navigation, Protocol for the Suppression of Unlawful Acts against the Safety of Fixed Platforms located on the Continental Shelf, International Convention for the Suppression of Terrorist Bombings, and the International Convention for the Suppression of the Financing of Terrorism (1999).

f) The phrase *those who finance terrorism* refers to any person, group, undertaking or other entity that provides or collects, by any means, directly or indirectly, funds or other assets that may be used, in full or in part, to facilitate the commission of terrorist acts, or to any persons or entities acting on behalf of, or at the direction of such persons, groups, undertakings or other entities. This includes those who provide or collect funds or other assets with the intention that they should be used or in the knowledge that they are to be used, in full or in part, in order to carry out terrorist acts.

g) The term *terrorist organisation* refers to any legal person, group, undertaking or other entity owned or controlled directly or indirectly by a terrorist(s).

h) The term *designated persons* refers to those persons or entities designated by the Al-Qaida and Taliban Sanctions Committee pursuant to S/RES/1267(1999) or those persons or entities designated and accepted, as appropriate, by jurisdictions pursuant to S/RES/1373(2001).

i) The phrase *without delay*, for the purposes of S/RES/1267(1999), means, ideally, within a matter of hours of a designation by the Al-Qaida and Taliban Sanctions Committee. For the purposes of S/RES/1373(2001), the phrase *without delay* means upon having reasonable grounds, or a reasonable basis, to suspect or believe that a person or entity is a terrorist, one who finances terrorism or a terrorist organisation. The phrase *without delay* should be interpreted in the context of the need to prevent the flight or dissipation of terrorist-linked funds or other assets, and the need for global, concerted action to interdict and disrupt their flow swiftly.

Freezing without delay terrorist-related funds or other assets

8. In order to fulfil the preventive intent of Special Recommendation III, jurisdictions should establish the necessary authority and adopt the following standards and procedures to freeze the funds or other assets of terrorists, those who finance terrorism and terrorist organisations in accordance with both S/RES/1267(1999) and S/RES/1373(2001):

a) Authority to freeze, unfreeze and prohibit dealing in funds or other assets of designated persons. Jurisdictions should prohibit by enforceable means the transfer, conversion, disposition or movement of funds or other assets. Options for providing the authority to freeze and unfreeze terrorist funds or other assets include:

i) empowering or designating a competent authority or a court to issue, administer and enforce freezing and unfreezing actions under relevant mechanisms, or *ii)* enacting legislation that places responsibility for freezing the funds or other assets of designated persons publicly identified by a competent authority or a court on the person or entity holding the funds or other assets and subjecting them to sanctions for non-compliance.

The authority to freeze and unfreeze funds or other assets should also extend to funds or other assets derived or generated from funds or other assets owned or controlled directly or indirectly by such terrorists, those who finance terrorism, or terrorist organisations.

Whatever option is chosen there should be clearly identifiable competent authorities responsible for enforcing the measures.

The competent authorities shall ensure that their nationals or any persons and entities within their territories are prohibited from making any funds or other assets, economic resources or financial or other related services available, directly or indirectly, wholly or jointly, for the benefit of: designated persons, terrorists; those who finance terrorism; terrorist organisations; entities owned or controlled, directly or indirectly, by such persons or entities; and persons and entities acting on behalf of or at the direction of such persons or entities.

b) Freezing procedures. Jurisdictions should develop and implement procedures to freeze the funds or other assets specified in paragraph *c)* below without delay and without giving prior notice to the persons or entities concerned. Persons or entities holding such funds or other assets should be required by law to freeze them and should furthermore be subject to sanctions for non-compliance with this requirement. Any delay between the official receipt of information provided in support of a designation and the actual freezing of the funds or other assets of designated persons undermines the effectiveness of designation by affording designated persons time to remove funds or other assets from identifiable accounts and places. Consequently, these procedures must ensure *i)* the prompt determination whether reasonable grounds or a reasonable basis exists to initiate an action under a freezing mechanism and *ii)* the subsequent freezing of funds or other assets without delay upon determination that such grounds or basis for freezing exist. Jurisdictions should develop efficient and effective systems for communicating actions taken under their freezing mechanisms to the financial sector immediately upon taking such action. As well, they should provide clear guidance, particularly financial institutions and other persons or entities that may be holding targeted funds or other assets on obligations in taking action under freezing mechanisms.

c) Funds or other assets to be frozen or, if appropriate, seized. Under Special Recommendation III, funds or other assets to be frozen include those subject to freezing under S/RES/1267(1999) and S/RES/1373(2001). Such funds or other assets would also include those wholly or jointly owned or controlled, directly or indirectly, by designated persons. In accordance with their obligations under the

United Nations International Convention for the Suppression of the Financing of Terrorism (1999) [the Terrorist Financing Convention (1999)], jurisdictions should be able to freeze or, if appropriate, seize any funds or other assets that they identify, detect, and verify, in accordance with applicable legal principles, as being used by, allocated for, or being made available to terrorists, those who finance terrorists or terrorist organisations. Freezing or seizing under the Terrorist Financing Convention (1999) may be conducted by freezing or seizing in the context of a criminal investigation or proceeding. Freezing action taken under Special Recommendation III shall be without prejudice to the rights of third parties acting in good faith.

d) De-listing and unfreezing procedures. Jurisdictions should develop and implement publicly known procedures to consider de-listing requests upon satisfaction of certain criteria consistent with international obligations and applicable legal principles, and to unfreeze the funds or other assets of de-listed persons or entities in a timely manner. For persons and entities designated under S/RES/1267(1999), such procedures and criteria should be in accordance with procedures adopted by the Al-Qaida and Taliban Sanctions Committee under S/RES/1267(1999).

e) Unfreezing upon verification of identity. For persons or entities with the same or similar name as designated persons, who are inadvertently affected by a freezing mechanism, jurisdictions should develop and implement publicly known procedures to unfreeze the funds or other assets of such persons or entities in a timely manner upon verification that the person or entity involved is not a designated person.

f) Providing access to frozen funds or other assets in certain circumstances. Where jurisdictions have determined that funds or other assets, which are otherwise subject to freezing pursuant to the obligations under S/RES/1267(1999), are necessary for basic expenses; for the payment of certain types of fees, expenses and service charges, or for extraordinary expenses,[7] jurisdictions should authorise access to such funds or other assets in accordance with the procedures set out in S/RES/1452(2002) and subject to approval of the Al-Qaida and Taliban Sanctions Committee. On the same grounds, jurisdictions may authorise access to funds or other assets, if freezing measures are applied pursuant to S/RES/1373(2001).

g) Remedies. Jurisdictions should provide for a mechanism through which a person or an entity that is the target of a freezing mechanism in the context of terrorist financing can challenge that measure with a view to having it reviewed by a competent authority or a court.

---

[7] See Article 1, S/RES/1452(2002) for the specific types of expenses that are covered.

h) Sanctions. Jurisdictions should adopt appropriate measures to monitor effectively the compliance with relevant legislation, rules or regulations governing freezing mechanisms by financial institutions and other persons or entities that may be holding funds or other assets as indicated in paragraph 8*c)* above. Failure to comply with such legislation, rules or regulations should be subject to civil, administrative or criminal sanctions.

Seizure and Confiscation

9. Consistent with FATF Recommendation 3, jurisdictions should adopt measures similar to those set forth in Article V of the United Nations Convention against Illicit Traffic in Narcotic Drugs and Psychotropic Substances (1988), Articles 12 to 14 of the United Nations Convention on Transnational Organised Crime (2000), and Article 8 of the Terrorist Financing Convention (1999), including legislative measures, to enable their courts or competent authorities to seize and confiscate terrorist funds or other assets.

Special Recommendation III: Freezing and Confiscating Terrorist Assets

Freezing Terrorist Assets[8]
International Best Practices

Introduction

Responding to the growing prevalence of terrorist attacks around the world, the international community united in a campaign to *freeze the funds or other assets*[9] of *terrorists, those who finance terrorism, and terrorist organisations* around the world. As part of this campaign, the United Nations Security Council issued resolutions S/RES/1267(1999) and S/RES/1373(2001). These international obligations are reiterated in FATF Special Recommendation III (SR III). The Interpretative Note to SR III (Interpretative Note) explains how these international freezing obligations should be fulfilled. To further assist in this effort, the FATF has identified the following set of best practices which are based on jurisdictions' experience to date and which may serve as a benchmark for developing institutional, legal, and procedural frameworks of an effective terrorist financing freezing regime.[10] These best practices are organised along

---

[8] The term "blocking" is a synonym of "freezing". These best practices will not address the funds or other asset seizure or funds or other asset confiscation / forfeiture authorities and procedures of a counter-terrorist financing regime, although the process of searching for such funds or other assets may be identical in cases of freezing, seizure and confiscation or forfeiture.

[9] Any term or phrase introduced in italics in this Best Practices Paper shall have the same meaning throughout as that ascribed to it in the Interpretative Note to FATF Special Recommendation III (SR III).

[10] These best practices focus on the financial sector because of the high risk of terrorist financing associated with this sector and also because of this sector's particular need for communication and guidance regarding the freezing of terrorist-related funds or other assets. However, the FATF recognises that all persons and entities are obligated to freeze the funds or other assets of persons designated under either S/RES/1267(1999) or S/RES/1373(2001). Additionally, S/RES/1373(2001) prohibits all persons and entities from providing any

five basic themes and complement the obligations set forth in the Interpretative Note. A common element to each of these themes is the importance of sharing terrorist financing information.

Importance of an Effective Freezing Regime

2. Effective freezing regimes are critical to combating the financing of terrorism and accomplish much more than freezing the terrorist-related funds or other assets present at any particular time. Effective freezing regimes also combat terrorism by:

i) deterring non-designated parties who might otherwise be willing to finance terrorist activity;

ii) exposing terrorist financing "money trails" that may generate leads to previously unknown terrorist cells and financiers;

iii) dismantling terrorist financing networks by encouraging designated persons to disassociate themselves from terrorist activity and renounce their affiliation with terrorist groups;

iv) terminating terrorist cash flows by shutting down the pipelines used to move terrorist-related funds or other assets;

v) forcing terrorists to use more costly and higher risk means of financing their activities, which makes them more susceptible to detection and disruption; and

vi) fostering international co-operation and compliance with obligations under S/RES/1267(1999) and S/RES/1373(2001).

3. Efforts to combat terrorist financing are greatly undermined if jurisdictions do not freeze the funds or other assets of designated persons quickly and effectively. Nevertheless, in determining the limits of or fostering widespread support for an effective counter-terrorist financing regime, jurisdictions must also respect human rights, respect the rule of law and recognise the rights of innocent third parties.

Statement of the Problem

4. The global nature of terrorist financing networks and the urgency of responding to terrorist threats require unprecedented levels of communication,

---

financial services or any form of support to any designated person. Any references to financial institutions should, therefore, be understood to include other relevant persons and entities.

co-operation and collaboration within and among governments, and between the public and private sectors. It is recognised that jurisdictions will necessarily adopt different terrorist financing freezing regimes in accordance with their differing legal traditions, constitutional requirements, systems of government and technological capabilities. However, the efficient and rapid dissemination of terrorist financing information to all those who can help identify, disrupt and dismantle terrorist financing networks must be a central focus of the international effort to freeze terrorist-related funds or other assets. Active participation and full support by the private sector is also essential to the success of any terrorist financing freezing regime. Consequently, jurisdictions should work with the private sector to ensure its ongoing co-operation in developing and implementing an effective terrorist-financing regime.

Best Practices

5. **Establishing effective regimes and competent authorities or courts.** Jurisdictions should establish the necessary legal authority and procedures, and designate accountable, competent authorities or courts responsible for: *a)* freezing the funds or other assets of designated persons; *b)* lifting such freezing action; and *c)* providing access to frozen funds or other assets in certain circumstances. Jurisdictions may undertake the following best practices to establish a comprehensive and effective terrorist financing freezing regime:

i) Develop a designation process which authorises a competent authority or a court to freeze funds or other assets based on information creating reasonable grounds, or a reasonable basis, to suspect or believe that such funds or other assets are terrorist-related. Jurisdictions may adopt executive, administrative or judicial procedures in this regard, provided that: *a)* a competent authority or a court is immediately available to determine whether reasonable grounds, or a reasonable basis, to suspect or believe that a person or entity is a terrorist, terrorist organisation or associated person or entity exits;[11] *b)* terrorist-related funds or other assets are frozen immediately upon a determination that such reasonable grounds, or a reasonable basis, to suspect or believe exists; and *c)* freezing occurs without prior notice to the parties whose funds or other assets are being frozen. These procedures may complement existing civil and/or criminal seizure and forfeiture laws, and other available judicial procedures.

ii) Establish effective procedures to facilitate communication, co-operation and collaboration among relevant governmental agencies and entities, as appropriate, during the designation process in order to: *a)* develop all available information to accurately identify designated persons (*e.g.* birth date, address,

---

[11] A designation by the Al-Qaida and Taliban Sanctions Committee constitutes, ipso facto, reasonable grounds, or a reasonable basis, to suspect or believe that a person or entity is a terrorist, terrorist organisation or an associated person or entity.

citizenship or passport number for individuals; locations, date and jurisdiction of incorporation, partnership or association for entities, etc.)[12], and *b)* consider and co-ordinate, as appropriate, any designation with other options and actions for addressing terrorists, terrorist organisations and associated persons and entities.

iii) Develop a process for financial institutions to communicate information concerning frozen funds or other assets (name, accounts, amounts) to the competent authorities or courts in their jurisdiction. Identify, assess the impact of, and amend, as necessary and to the extent possible, existing bank secrecy provisions or data protection rules that may prohibit this communication to appropriate authorities of information concerning frozen terrorist-related funds or other assets.

iv) Identify and accommodate the concerns of the intelligence community, law enforcement, private sector and legal systems arising from circulation of sensitive information concerning frozen terrorist-related funds or other assets.

v) Develop a publicly known delisting process for considering any new arguments or evidence that may negate the basis for freezing funds or other assets[13] and develop procedures for reviewing the appropriateness of a freezing action upon presentation of any such new information.

vi) Develop procedures to ensure that adequate prohibitions against the publication of sensitive information exist in accordance with applicable legislation.

vii) Develop procedures and designate competent authorities or courts responsible for providing access to frozen funds or other assets in accordance with S/RES/1452(2002) to mitigate, where appropriate and feasible, unintended consequences of freezing action.

viii) Consider enacting hold-harmless or public indemnity[14] laws to shield financial institutions, their personnel, government officials, and other

---

[12] Accurate identification of a designated person is a precondition to an effective terrorist financing freezing regime.

[13] Only the Al-Qaida and Taliban Sanctions Committee can delist persons designated pursuant to S/RES/1267(1999).

[14] In contrast to hold-harmless laws, public indemnity laws allow a remedy for innocent parties that are injured by the good faith implementation of a terrorist financing freezing regime. The appropriate compensation or relief for such innocent parties is not at the expense of the persons or entities that actually implement the terrorist financing regime in good faith, but comes from a public insurance fund or similar vehicle established or made available by the applicable jurisdiction.

appropriate persons from legal liability when acting in good faith according to applicable law to implement the requirements of a terrorist financing freezing regime.

6. **Facilitating communication and co-operation with foreign governments and international institutions.** To the extent legally and constitutionally possible, jurisdictions may undertake the following best practices to improve international co-operation and the effectiveness of the international campaign against terrorist financing by sharing information relating to the freezing of terrorist-related funds or other assets:

i) Develop a system for mutual, early, and rapid pre-notification of pending designations, through diplomatic and other appropriate channels, where security concerns and applicable legal principles permit, to those jurisdictions invited to join in a designation and/or where funds or other assets of designated persons might be located, so that funds or other assets can be frozen simultaneously across jurisdictions with the objective of preventing terrorists, terrorist organisations and associated persons and entities from hiding or moving them. In this regard, consideration should be given to establishing a list of relevant contacts to ensure that freezing action is taken rapidly.[15]

ii) Develop a system for undertaking useful and appropriate consultation with other jurisdictions for the purpose of gathering, verifying, and correcting identifier information for designated persons as well as, where appropriate and where intelligence concerns and applicable laws permit, the sharing and development of information on possible terrorists and terrorist financing activity of the parties involved. In undertaking such consultation, jurisdictions should consider: *a)* the greater effectiveness of freezing on the basis of accurate and complete identifying information; *b)* the burden created by unsubstantiated or incomplete identifying information; *c)* the security concerns associated with releasing sensitive identifier or corroborating information; and *d)* the degree of danger or urgency associated with the potential designated persons. Where appropriate such information should be shared and developed before a designation is made.

iii) Prepare a packet of information for each potential designation that includes as much information as is available and appropriate to identify the designated person accurately and to set forth the basis for the potential designation in any pre-notification or communication of the designation (*see Paragraph 6.i), above*).

---

[15] Such a pre-notification system should be developed to compliment rather than replace the pre-notification system in place for submitting designations to the Al-Qaida and Taliban Sanctions Committee and should include designations arising from obligations under S/RES/1373(2001).

iv) Develop a process for rapidly and globally communicating new designations and the accompanying packet of information to other jurisdictions.

v) Expand coverage of the hold-harmless and public indemnity laws referred to in *Paragraph 5.(viii)* above, or otherwise implement procedures to deal with situations in which freezing does not occur simultaneously, so as to avoid conflicting legal obligations for financial institutions that operate in multiple jurisdictions.

vi) Share on a mutual and confidential basis, to the extent possible, with other jurisdictions information about the amount of funds or other assets frozen pursuant to terrorist financing freezing orders by account.

vii) Make public and update on a regular basis the aggregate amount of funds or other assets frozen in order to signal the effectiveness of terrorist financing freezing regimes and to deter terrorist financing.

7. **Facilitating communication with the private sector.** Because terrorist-related funds or other assets overwhelmingly are held in the private sector, jurisdictions must develop efficient and effective means of communicating terrorist financing-related information with the general public, particularly financial institutions. To the extent possible and practicable, jurisdictions can adopt the following practices to develop and enhance communication with the private sector regarding the freezing of terrorist-related funds or other assets, the availability of additional information concerning existing designations, and other counter-terrorist financing guidance or instruction:

i) Integrate, organise, publish and update *without delay* the designated persons list, for example both alphabetically and by date of designation to assist financial institutions in freezing terrorist-related funds or other assets and making the list as user-friendly as possible. Create different entries for different aliases or different spellings of names. Where technologically possible provide a consolidated list in an electronic format with a clear indication of changes and additions. Consult the private sector on other details of the format of the list and co-ordinate the format internationally with other jurisdictions.

ii) Develop clear guidance to the private sector, particularly financial institutions, with respect to their obligations in freezing terrorist-related funds or other assets.

iii) Identify all financial institutions for use in notification and regulatory oversight and enforcement of freezing action related to terrorist financing, utilising, where appropriate and feasible, existing registration or licensing information.

iv) Implement a process for early, rapid and secure pre-notification of pending designations, where security concerns or applicable legal principles permit, to those financial institutions where funds or other assets of designated persons are known or believed to be located so that those institutions can freeze such funds or other assets immediately upon designation.

v) Implement a system for early, rapid, and uniform global communication, consistent with available technology and resources and where security concerns permit, of any designation-related information, amendments or revocations of designations. For the reasons set out in *Paragraph 6.(ii)* above, include as much information as is available and appropriate to clearly identify designated persons in any communication of a designation to the private sector.

vi) Implement a clear process for responding to inquiries concerning potential identification mismatches based on homonyms or similar sounding names.

vii) Develop appropriate regulatory authorities and procedures where applicable, and properly identify a point of contact to assist financial institutions in freezing terrorist-related funds or other assets and to address, where feasible, unforeseen or unintended consequences resulting from freezing action (such as the handling and disposition of perishable or wasting funds or other assets and authorising access to funds or other assets in accordance with S/RES/1452(2002)).

viii) Elaborate clear guidance to the private sector with respect to any permitted transactions in administering frozen funds or other assets (*e.g.* bank charges, fees, interest payments, crediting on frozen accounts, etc.).

8. **Ensuring adequate compliance, controls, and reporting in the private sector.**

Jurisdictions may work with the private sector in developing the following practices to: *a)* facilitate co-operation and compliance by the private sector in identifying and freezing funds or other assets of designated persons, and *b)* prevent designated persons from conducting financial or other transactions within their territories or through their financial institutions:[16]

i) Co-operate with the private sector generally and financial institutions in particular, especially those that are independently implementing programmes to prevent potential terrorist financing activity or those that have come forward with potentially incriminating information, in investigating possible financial activity by a designated person.

ii) Ensure that financial institutions develop and maintain adequate internal controls (including due diligence procedures and training programmes as appropriate) to identify the existing accounts, transactions, funds or other assets of designated persons.

---

[16] Many of the best practices set forth in this section reinforce obligations of jurisdictions and financial institutions under the revised FATF 40 Recommendations. As with all of the best practices set forth in this paper, these best practices should be interpreted and implemented in accordance with the revised FATF 40 Recommendations.

iii) Ensure that financial institutions immediately freeze any identified funds or other assets held or controlled by designated persons.

iv) Ensure that financial institutions have the appropriate procedures and resources to meet there obligations under SR III.

v) Ensure that financial institutions implement reasonable procedures to prevent designated persons from conducting transactions with, in or through them.

vi) Develop an effective monitoring system by a competent authority or a court with sufficient supervisory experience, authority and resources with a mandate to support the objectives set out in *Paragraphs 8.ii), iii) and iv)* above.

vii) Encourage, to the extent commercially reasonable, financial institutions to search or examine past financial activity by designated persons.

viii) Identify, assess compliance with, and improve as necessary client or customer identification rules used by financial institutions.

ix) Identify, assess compliance with, and improve as necessary record keeping requirements of financial institutions.

x) Adopt reasonable measures to consider beneficial owners, signatories and power of attorney with respect to accounts or transactions held by financial institutions when searching for activity by designated persons, including any ongoing business relationships.

xi) Harmonise counter-terrorist financing internal controls within each economic sector, as appropriate, with anti-money laundering programmes.

9. Ensuring thorough follow-up investigation, co-ordination with law enforcement, intelligence and security authorities, and appropriate feedback to the private sector. Financial information pertaining to designated persons is extremely valuable to law enforcement and other security authorities investigating terrorist financing networks. Law enforcement and prosecutorial authorities should, therefore, be given access to such information. Jurisdictions may adopt the following practices to ensure that information available from the private sector in freezing terrorist-related funds or other assets is fully exploited:

i) Develop procedures to ensure that appropriate intelligence and law enforcement bodies and authorities receive, share, and act on information gathered from the private sector's freezing of terrorist-related funds or other assets, including sharing such information internationally to the extent possible and appropriate.

ii) Develop procedures to ensure that, to the extent possible and appropriate, law enforcement authorities provide feedback to financial institutions indicating how financial intelligence is being used to support law enforcement actions.

iii) Gather and analyse all available terrorist financing data to: *a)* assess terrorist financing activity; *b)* determine terrorist financing trends; *c)* develop and share terrorist financing typologies, including sharing such information internationally as appropriate; *d)* identify vulnerable sectors within each jurisdiction, and *e)* take appropriate measures to safeguard any such vulnerable sectors.

Special Recommendation VI: Alternative Remittance

Interpretative Note

General

1. Money or value transfer systems have shown themselves vulnerable to misuse for money laundering and terrorist financing purposes. The objective of Special Recommendation VI is to increase the transparency of payment flows by ensuring that jurisdictions impose consistent anti-money laundering and counter-terrorist financing measures on all forms of money/value transfer systems, particularly those traditionally operating outside the conventional financial sector and not currently subject to the FATF Recommendations. This Recommendation and Interpretative Note underscore the need to bring all money or value transfer services, whether formal or informal, within the ambit of certain minimum legal and regulatory requirements in accordance with the relevant FATF Recommendations.

2. Special Recommendation VI consists of three core elements:

a. jurisdictions should require licensing or registration of persons (natural or legal) that provide money/value transfer services, including through informal systems;

b. jurisdictions should ensure that money/value transmission services, including informal systems (as described in paragraph 5 below), are subject to applicable FATF Forty Recommendations (2003) (in particular, Recommendations 4-16 and 21-25)[17] and the Eight Special Recommendations (in particular SR VII); and

c. jurisdictions should be able to impose sanctions on money/value transfer services, including informal systems, that operate without a license or registration and that fail to comply with relevant FATF Recommendations.

---

[17] When this Interpretative Note was originally issued, these references were to the 1996 FATF Forty Recommendations. Subsequent to the publication of the revised FATF Forty Recommendations in June 2003, this text was updated accordingly. All references are now to the 2003 FATF Forty Recommendations.

Scope and Application

3. For the purposes of this Recommendation, the following definitions are used:

4. *Money or value transfer service* refers to a financial service that accepts cash, cheques, other monetary instruments or other stores of value in one location and pays a corresponding sum in cash or other form to a beneficiary in another location by means of a communication, message, transfer or through a clearing network to which the money/value transfer service belongs. Transactions performed by such services can involve one or more intermediaries and a third party final payment.

5. A money or value transfer service may be provided by persons (natural or legal) formally through the regulated financial system or informally through non-bank financial institutions or other business entities or any other mechanism either through the regulated financial system (for example, use of bank accounts) or through a network or mechanism that operates outside the regulated system. In some jurisdictions, informal systems are frequently referred to as *alternative remittance services* or *underground (or parallel) banking systems*. Often these systems have ties to particular geographic regions and are therefore described using a variety of specific terms. Some examples of these terms include *hawala, hundi, fei-chien*, and the *black market peso exchange*.[18]

6. *Licensing* means a requirement to obtain permission from a designated competent authority in order to operate a money/value transfer service legally.

7. *Registration* in this Recommendation means a requirement to register with or declare to a designated competent authority the existence of a money/value transfer service in order for the business to operate legally.

8. The obligation of licensing or registration applies to agents. At a minimum, the principal business must maintain a current list of agents which must be made available to the designated competent authority. An *agent* is any person who provides money or value transfer service under the direction of or by contract with a legally registered or licensed remitter (for example, licensees, franchisees, concessionaires).

---

[18] The inclusion of these examples does not suggest that such systems are legal in any particular jurisdiction.

Applicability of Special Recommendation VI

9. Special Recommendation VI should apply to all persons (natural or legal), which conduct for or on behalf of another person (natural or legal) the types of activity described in paragraphs 4 and 5 above as a primary or substantial part of their business or when such activity is undertaken on a regular or recurring basis, including as an ancillary part of a separate business enterprise.

10. Jurisdictions need not impose a separate licensing/registration system or designate another competent authority in respect to persons (natural or legal) already licensed or registered as financial institutions (as defined by the FATF Forty Recommendations (2003)) within a particular jurisdiction, which under such license or registration are permitted to perform activities indicated in paragraphs 4 and 5 above and which are already subject to the full range of applicable obligations under the FATF Forty Recommendations (2003) (in particular, Recommendations 4-16 and 21-25) and the Eight Special Recommendations (in particular SR VII).

Licensing or Registration and Compliance

11. Jurisdictions should designate an authority to grant licences and/or carry out registration and ensure that the requirement is observed. There should be an authority responsible for ensuring compliance by money/value transfer services with the FATF Recommendations (including the Eight Special Recommendations). There should also be effective systems in place for monitoring and ensuring such compliance. This interpretation of Special Recommendation VI (*i.e.*, the need for designation of competent authorities) is consistent with FATF Recommendation 23.

Sanctions

12. Persons providing money/value transfer services without a license or registration should be subject to appropriate administrative, civil or criminal sanctions.[19] Licensed or registered money/value transfer services which fail to comply fully with the relevant measures called for in the FATF Forty Recommendations (2003) or the Eight Special Recommendations should also be subject to appropriate sanctions.

---

[19] Jurisdictions may authorise temporary or provisional operation of money/value transfer services that are already in existence at the time of implementing this Special Recommendation to permit such services to obtain a license or to register.

SPECIAL RECOMMENDATION VI: ALTERNATIVE REMITTANCE

COMBATING THE ABUSE OF ALTERNATIVE REMITTANCE SYSTEMS

INTERNATIONAL BEST PRACTICES[20]

Introduction

1. Alternative remittance systems are financial services, traditionally operating outside the conventional financial sector, where value or funds are moved from one geographic location to another.

Special Recommendation VI: Alternative Remittance[21]
Each country should take measures to ensure that persons or legal entities, including agents, that provide a service for the transmission of money or value, including transmission through an informal money or value transfer system or network, should be licensed or registered and subject to all the FATF Recommendations that apply to banks and non-bank financial institutions. Each country should ensure that persons or legal entities that carry out this service illegally are subject to administrative, civil or criminal sanctions.

2. While the Interpretative Note is intended to further explain Special Recommendation VI, the Best Practices Paper is intended to give additional details (including some examples), to offer jurisdictions suggestions in implementing Special Recommendation VI and to give them guidance on how to detect alternative remittance systems outside the conventional financial sector. It focuses on many practical issues, such as the identification of money/value transfer services, the procedures for licensing or registering such services and

---

[20] The content of this paper is taken primarily from APG's Draft Alternative Remittance Regulation Implementation Package (Oct 2002.) This Best Practices Paper is intended to draw on the work of the APG Working Group on Underground Banking and Alternative Remittance Systems into international best practices.

[21] See also the FATF Interpretative Note to Special Recommendation VI: Alternative Remittance.

their customer due diligence procedures. This Best Practices Paper addresses the following topics:

- Definition of *money or value transfer service*
- Statement of Problem
- Principles
- Areas of Focus

    i) Licensing/Registration

        a. Requirement to Register or License

        b. Applications for Licence

        c. Business Address

        d. Accounts

    ii) Identification and Awareness Raising

        a. Identification Strategies

        b. Awareness Raising Campaigns

    iii) Anti-Money Laundering Regulations

        a. Customer Identification

        b. Record Keeping Requirement

        c. Suspicious Transaction Reporting

    iv) Compliance Monitoring

    v) Sanctions

Definition

3. Throughout this Best Practices Paper, the following definition from the Interpretative Note to SR VI is used.

4. *Money or value transfer service* (MVT service) refers to a financial service that accepts cash, cheques, other monetary instruments or other stores of value in one location and pays a corresponding sum in cash or other form to a beneficiary in another location by means of a communication, message, transfer or through a clearing network to which the MVT service belongs. Transactions performed by such services can involve one or more intermediaries and a third party final payment.

5. A MVT service may be provided by persons (natural or legal) formally through the regulated financial system or informally through entities that operate outside the regulated system. In some jurisdictions, informal systems are frequently referred to as *alternative remittance services* or *underground (or parallel) banking systems*. Often these systems have ties to particular geographic regions and are therefore described using a variety of specific terms. Some examples of these terms include *hawala, hundi, fei-chien*, and the *black market peso exchange*.

Statement of Problem

6. As "Know Your Customer" and other anti-money laundering strategies come into operation in the formal financial sector, money laundering activity may be displaced to other sectors. Jurisdictions have reported increased money laundering activity using the non-bank sector and non-financial businesses. Measures should therefore be taken to obviate any increased abuse of the unregulated sector. MVT services are increasingly vulnerable to abuse by money launderers and the financiers of terrorism, particularly when their operations are conducted through informal systems involving non-bank financial institutions or other business entities not subject to the applicable obligations under the FATF Recommendations.

7. In addition to their use by legitimate clients, criminals have laundered the proceeds of various criminal activities using MVT services. Primarily, unregulated MVT services permit funds to be sent anonymously, allowing the money launderer or terrorist financier to freely send funds without having to identify himself or herself. In some cases, few or no records are kept. In other cases, records may be kept, but are inaccessible to authorities. The lack of adequate records makes it extremely difficult, if not impossible, to trace the funds after the transaction has been completed.

8. From recent research, it is suspected that the principal criminal activities engaged in by those who utilise MVT services are the illicit trafficking in narcotic drugs and psychotropic substances, illicit arms trafficking, corruption, evasion of government taxes and duties, trafficking in human beings and migrant smuggling. Recent reports indicate that international terrorist groups have used MVT services to transmit funds for the purpose of funding terrorist activities. (For example, investigation of the September 11, 2001 terrorist attacks has found that both the formal financial sector and informal MVT services were used to transfer money to the terrorists.)

Principles

9. The following principles guide the establishment of these best practices:

- In certain jurisdictions, informal MVT services provide a legitimate and efficient service. Their services are particularly relevant where access to the formal financial sector is difficult or prohibitively expensive. Informal MVT services are available outside the normal banking business hours. Furthermore, money can be sent to and from locations where the formal banking system does not operate.
- Informal MVT services are more entrenched in some regions than others for cultural and other reasons. Underground banking is a long-standing tradition in many countries and pre-dates the spread of Western banking systems in the 19th and 20th centuries. These services operate primarily to provide transfer facilities to neighbouring jurisdictions for expatriate workers repatriating funds. However, the staging posts of underground banking are no longer confined to those regions where they have their historical roots. Accordingly, informal MVT services are no longer used solely by persons from specific ethnic or cultural backgrounds.
- MVT services can take on a variety of forms which, in addition to the adoption of a risk-based approach to the problem, points to the need to take a functional, rather than a legalistic definition. Accordingly, the FATF has developed suggested practices that would best aid authorities to reduce the likelihood that MVT services will be misused or exploited by money launderers and the financiers of terrorism.
- Government oversight should be flexible, effective, and proportional to the risk of abuse. Mechanisms that minimise the compliance burden, without creating loopholes for money launderers and terrorist financiers and without being so burdensome that it in effect causes MVT services to go "underground" making them even harder to detect should be given due consideration.
- It is acknowledged that in some jurisdictions informal MVT services have been banned. Special Recommendation VI does not seek legitimisation of informal MVT services in those jurisdictions. The identification and awareness raising issues noted may however be of use for competent authorities involved in identifying informal MVT services and for sanctioning those who operate illegally.

Areas of Focus

10. Analysis of the investigations and law-enforcement activities of various jurisdictions indicate several ways in which informal MVT services have been abused by terrorists and launderers and suggests areas in which preventive measures should be considered.

i) Licensing/Registration

11. A core element of Special Recommendation VI is that jurisdictions should require licensing or registration of persons (natural or legal) that provide informal MVT services. The FATF defines these terms in its interpretative note to Special Recommendation VI. A key element of both registration and licensing is the requirement that the relevant regulatory body is aware of the existence of the business. The key difference between the two is that licensing implies that the regulatory body has inspected and sanctioned the particular operator to conduct such a business whereas registration means that the operator has been entered into the regulator's list of operators.

a. Requirement to Register or License

- At a minimum, jurisdictions should ensure that MVT services are required to register with a designated competent authority such as a Financial Intelligence Unit (FIU) or financial sector regulatory body. Registration of MVT services is likely to be a relatively cost effective approach when compared to the significant resources required for licensing.

- The obligation of licensing or registration applies to agents. At a minimum, the principal business must maintain a current list of agents which must be made available to the designated competent authority. An agent is any person who provides MVT service under the direction of or by contract with a legally registered or licensed MVT service (for example, licensees, franchisees, concessionaires.

b. Applications for Licence

- In determining whether an application for licensing can be accepted by the regulatory authority, it is clear that some form of scrutiny of the application and the operator needs to be conducted. This is in line with FATF Recommendation 23[22] which states that regulators should introduce "*the necessary legal or regulatory measures to prevent criminals or their associates from holding or being the beneficial owner of a significant or controlling interest or holding a management function in a financial institution.*"

- Authorities should conduct background checks on the operators, owners, directors and shareholders of MVT services. When considering the suitability of a potential operator, the authorities should conduct a criminal record check

---

[22] When this Best Practices Paper was originally issued, these references were to the 1996 FATF Forty Recommendations. Subsequent to the publication of the revised FATF Forty Recommendations in June 2003, this text was updated accordingly. All references are now to the 2003 FATF Forty Recommendations.

on the principal persons having control over the operations of the MVT service, as well as consult appropriate law enforcement databases, including suspicious or unusual reporting filings. Consideration should be given to defining the type of criminal record which would make the applicant ineligible to operate a licensed MVT service.

c. Business Address

- MVT services should be required to submit details of the addresses from which they operate and to notify the authorities upon any change of address or cessation of business. Where possible, this information may be made available to both the public so they may check which MVT service is properly licensed or registered before using their services, and to investigative/regulatory authorities during the course of their work. This also has value for financial institutions with which the MVT services maintain accounts as they are able to identify which MVT services are licensed/registered and thus are more able to identify illegal operators and to report to the FIU or appropriate competent authority accordingly.

d. Accounts

- In processing cash and in the settlement of transactions, MVT services use bank accounts. Some operators run a number of businesses, of which MVT service is one, and use business accounts to conduct or conceal the remittances of funds on behalf of their clients thereby masking the true origin of the commingled funds and accounts.

- MVT services should maintain the name and address of any depository institution with which the operator maintains a transaction account for the purpose of the MVT service business. These accounts must be capable of being identified and should be held in the name of the registered/licensed entity so that the accounts and the register or list of licensed entities can be easily cross-referenced.

- Traditional financial institutions should be encouraged to develop more detailed understanding as to how MVT services utilise bank accounts to conduct their operations, particularly when accounts are used in the settlement process.

ii) Identification and Awareness Raising

12. Some informal MVT services are not known to regulatory and enforcement agencies, which makes them attractive to the financiers of terrorism. Identification of these MVT services will make it less attractive for criminal and terrorist groups to use them to facilitate and hide the financing of their activities.

13. For the majority of jurisdictions, proactive identification of informal MVT services is an integral element of establishing and maintaining an effective registration/licensing regime. Once informal MVT services have been located, compliance programmes can be instituted under which the agents are approached, their details are recorded and they are provided information as to their obligations. Once regulatory regimes are in place, ongoing compliance work will include strategies to identify those MVT services not yet known to regulatory authorities. Jurisdictions may apply a range of strategies to uncover MVT services, using a number of approaches concurrently. Jurisdictions are encouraged to foster close co-ordination within the relevant authorities for the purposes of developing inter-agency strategies and using available resources to identify MVT services that may be operating illegally. Below is a list of suggested best practices for identifying MVT services and raising public awareness about their activities. As best practices, it is recognized that some of these suggestions may not be appropriate for every jurisdiction and that each jurisdiction must develop strategies best suited to its individual system.

a. Identification Strategies

14. Best practices in the area of identification strategies include:

- Examining the full range of media to detect advertising conducted by informal MVT services and informing operators of their registration/licensing obligations. This includes national, local and community newspapers, radio and the Internet; giving particular attention to the printed media in various communities; and monitoring activities in certain neighbourhoods or areas where informal MVT services may be operating.

- During investigations, information about informal MVT services may be uncovered which should be passed on to the competent authorities. Best practices include encouraging investigators to pay particular attention to ledgers of business that may be associated with informal MVT services; encouraging enforcement agencies to look for patterns of activity that might indicate involvement of informal MVT services; and, where possible, encouraging enforcement agencies to consider using undercover techniques or other specific investigative techniques to detect MVT services that may be operating illegally.

- Consulting with the operators of registered/licensed MVT services for potential leads on MVT services that are unregistered or unlicensed.

- Being aware that informal MVT services are often utilised where there is bulk currency moved internationally, particularly when couriers are involved. Paying particular attention to the origin and owners of any such currency. Couriers could provide insights for the identification and potential prosecution of illegal operators with whom the couriers are associated, especially when potential violations by couriers are linked back to the source of the informal MVT service operation.

- Paying particular attention to domestic suspicious transaction or unusual activity reporting, as well as to domestic and international large value cash reporting, to identify possible links to informal MVT services.

- Assisting banks and other financial institutions in developing an understanding of what activities/indicators are suggestive of informal MVT service operations and using this to identify them. Many informal MVT services maintain bank accounts and conduct transactions in the formal financial sector as part of other business operations. Giving banks the authority to crosscheck particular accounts against a register of these operators and notify the relevant regulatory authority as appropriate.

- Once informal MVT services are identified international exchange of information and intelligence on these entities between the relevant bodies can be facilitated. Consideration could be given to sharing domestic registers with international counterparts. This strategy would also assist jurisdictions to identify local operators not previously known.

b. Awareness Raising Campaigns

15. Best practices in the area of awareness raising campaigns include:

- Making informal MVT services aware of their obligations to license or register, as well as any other obligations with which they may have to comply. Ensuring that the competent authorities responsible for overseeing and/or registering or licensing informal MVT services know how to detect those services that have not registered or been licensed. Finally, ensuring that law enforcement is aware of the compliance requirements for MVT services in addition to the methods by which those services are used for illicit purposes.

- Using education and compliance programmes, including visits to businesses which may be operating informal MVT services to advise them of licensing or registration and reporting obligations, as opportunities to seek information about others in their industry. Using these outreach efforts by law enforcement and regulatory agencies to enhance their understanding about the operations, record-keeping functions and customer bases of informal MVT services. Extending outreach campaigns to businesses typically servicing informal MVT services (such as shipping services, courier services and trading companies). Placing in trade journals, newspapers or other publications of general distribution notices of the need for informal MVT services to register or license and file reports.

- Ensuring that the full range of training, awareness opportunities and other forms of education are provided to investigators with information about MVT services, their obligations under the regulatory regime and ways in which their services can be used by money launderers and terrorist financiers. This information can be provided through training courses, presentations at seminars and conferences, articles in policing journals and other publications.

- Issuing various financial sector publications of guidelines to encourage licensing or registration and reporting and also general material to ensure financial institutions currently subject to suspicious transaction reporting requirements develop an understanding of MVT services. (Also see section on suspicious transaction reporting on page 11.) Informing potential customers about the risks of utilising illegal MVT services and their role in financing of terrorism and money laundering.

- Requiring entities to display their registration/license to customers once they are registered/licensed. Legitimate clients will likely have a higher degree of confidence in using registered/licensed operators and may therefore seek out those operators displaying such documentation.

- Making a list of all licensed or registered persons that provide MVT services publicly available.

iii) Anti-Money Laundering Regulations

16. The second element of Special Recommendation VI is that jurisdictions should ensure MVT services are subject to FATF Recommendations 4-16 and 21-25 and also to the Eight Special Recommendations.

17. There is key information that both regulatory and enforcement bodies need access to if they are to conduct effective investigations of money laundering and terrorist financing involving MVT services. Essentially, agencies need the information about the customers, the transactions themselves, any suspicious transactions, the MVT service's location and the accounts used. The MVT service must also have further records on hand available to regulatory and enforcement bodies as needed.

18. It is considered that to be effective in addressing the problem of MVT services, regulations should not be overly restrictive. Regulation must allow for those who abuse these systems to be found and stopped, but it should not be so burdensome that it in effect causes the systems to go "underground", making it even harder to uncover money laundering and terrorist financing through alternative remittance.

a. Customer Identification

19. The principle of Know Your Customer ("KYC") has been the backbone of anti-money laundering and counter terrorist financing measures which have been introduced to financial service providers in recent years, and this should also be the case for the MVT service sector. Customer identification

requirements in the formal financial sector have had a deterrent effect, causing a shift in money laundering activities to other sectors. FATF Recommendations 4-10 and 12 concern customer identification and record keeping.

- FATF's Recommendation 5 is considered to be the minimum effective level which MVT services should be required to fulfil. The current recommendation sets out that the institution should be "*identifying the customer and verifying that customer's identity using reliable, independent source documents, data or information*". The documents commonly acknowledged and accepted for identification purposes are identity card, passport, drivers' license or social security card. It is important for the credibility of the system that failure to produce an acceptable form of identification will mean that a client will be rejected, the transaction will not be conducted and, under specific circumstances, a suspicious transaction report will be made.

- Proof of identity should be required when establishing a business relationship with the MVT service whether the relationship is a short term *i.e.* a single transaction, or a long term one. Transactions via phone, fax or Internet should only be conducted after customer identification complying with FATF Recommendation 5 has occurred (*i.e.*, a business relationship has already been established). If the client's identification has not been previously established, then the transaction should not be processed.[23]

b. Record Keeping Requirement

20. Investigative agencies need to be able to retrace transactions and identify persons effecting the transactions (*i.e.* the audit trail) if they are to successfully investigate money laundering and terrorist financing. The requirement for MVT services to maintain records is essential for effective regulation of the field, but it is this area in which the balance between the regulator's needs and the burden on the operator most clearly needs to be struck.

- Jurisdictions should consider FATF's Special Recommendation VII on Wire Transfers[24] when developing guidance in this area. This recommendation specifically deals with funds transfers, including those made through MVT

---

[23] See footnote 3.

[24] Text of SRVII: Countries should take measures to require financial institutions, including money remitters, to include accurate and meaningful originator information (name, address and account number) on funds transfers and related messages that are sent, and the information should remain with the transfer or related message through the payment chain. Countries should take measures to ensure that financial institutions, including money remitters, conduct enhanced scrutiny of and monitor for suspicious activity funds transfers which do not contain complete originator information (name, address and account number).

services. It should be noted that Special Recommendation VI covers the transmission of "value" as well as money.

- MVT services should comply with FATF Recommendation 10 to maintain, for at least five years, all necessary records on transactions both domestic and international. Jurisdictions should consider setting some minimum requirements for the form in which the records should be kept. Because records associated with MVT transfer services may often be coded and/or difficult to access, jurisdictions should also establish minimum standards for ensuring that they are intelligible and retrievable.

c. Suspicious Transaction Reporting

21. To maintain consistency with the obligations imposed on other financial institutions, jurisdictions should introduce transaction reporting in line with their current reporting requirements for financial institutions.

- Jurisdictions may consider issuing specific guidance as to what may constitute a suspicious transaction to the MVT service industry. Some currently used indicators of suspicious financial activity, such as those found in the FATF's Guidance for Financial Institutions in Detecting Terrorist Financing, are likely to be relevant for money/value transfer service activity. However, particular activities and indicators that are unique to this sector should be further developed.

- The second half of FATF's Special Recommendation VII on Wire Transfers should also be taken into account when developing guidance in this area. For example, operators that receive funds/value should ensure that the necessary originator information is included. The lack of complete originator information may be considered as a factor in assessing whether a transaction is suspicious and, as appropriate, whether it is thus required to be reported to the Financial Intelligence Unit or other competent authorities. If this information is not included, the operator should report suspicious activity to the local FIU or other competent authority if appropriate.

iv) Compliance Monitoring

22. Regulatory authorities need to monitor the sector with a view to identifying illegal operators and use of these facilities by criminal and terrorist groups. Jurisdictions are encouraged to consider the following options:

- Competent authorities should also be entitled to check on unregistered entities that are suspected to be involved in MVT services. There should be an effective process for using this authority.

- Granting regulatory agencies or supervisory authorities the authority to check the operations of a MVT service and make unexpected visits to operators to allow for the checking of the register's details and the inspection of records. Record keeping practices should be given particular attention.

- Establishing a process of identifying and classifying operators which are considered to be of high risk. In this context, "high risk" means those operators which are considered to be of high risk of being used to carry out money laundering or terrorist financing activities. Jurisdictions are encouraged to give such high risk entities extra attention from supervising authorities.

v) Sanctions

23. In designing legislation to address this problem, one of the aspects to be considered concerns the sanctions which are available to redress non-compliance. If a MVT service operator is found to be non-compliant with the relevant requirements of the legislation the competent authorities would be expected to sanction the operator. Ideally, jurisdictions should set up a system to employ civil, criminal or administrative sanctions depending on the severity of the offence. For instance, in some cases a warning may initially suffice. However, if a MVT service continues to be in non-compliance, it should receive stronger measures. There should be particularly strong penalties for MVT services and their operators that knowingly act against the law, for example by not registering.

24. To monitor the continued suitability of an individual to conduct a MVT service, jurisdictions are encouraged to put systems into place which would bring any conviction of an operator, shareholder or director following licensing or registration, to the attention of the appropriate authorities. Consideration should be given to defining the type of criminal record which would make the applicant ineligible to be a MVT service provider.

Special Recommendation VII: Wire Transfers

Interpretative Note[25]

Objective

1. Special Recommendation VII (SR VII) was developed with the objective of preventing terrorists and other criminals from having unfettered access to wire transfers for moving their funds and for detecting such misuse when it occurs. Specifically, it aims to ensure that basic information on the originator of wire transfers is immediately available 1) to appropriate law enforcement and/or prosecutorial authorities to assist them in detecting, investigating, prosecuting terrorists or other criminals and tracing the assets of terrorists or other criminals, 2) to financial intelligence units for analysing suspicious or unusual activity and disseminating it as necessary, and 3) to beneficiary financial institutions to facilitate the identification and reporting of suspicious transactions. It is not the intention of the FATF to impose rigid standards or to mandate a single operating process that would negatively affect the payment system.

Definitions

2. For the purposes of this interpretative note, the following definitions apply.

a. The terms *wire transfer* and *funds transfer* refer to any transaction carried out on behalf of an originator person (both natural and legal) through a financial institution by electronic means with a view to making an amount of money available to a beneficiary person at another financial institution. The originator and the beneficiary may be the same person.

b. Cross-border transfer means any wire transfer where the originator and beneficiary institutions are located in different jurisdictions. This term also refers to any chain of wire transfers that has at least one cross-border element.

---

[25] It is recognised that jurisdictions will need time to make relevant legislative or regulatory changes and to allow financial institutions to make necessary adaptations to their systems and procedures. This period should not be longer than two years after the adoption of this Interpretative Note.

c. Domestic transfer means any wire transfer where the originator and beneficiary institutions are located in the same jurisdiction. This term therefore refers to any chain of wire transfers that takes place entirely within the borders of a single jurisdiction, even though the system used to effect the wire transfer may be located in another jurisdiction.

d. The term financial institution is as defined by the FATF Forty Recommendations (2003).[26] The term does not apply to any persons or entities that provide financial institutions solely with message or other support systems for transmitting funds.[27]

e. The *originator* is the account holder, or where there is no account, the person (natural or legal) that places the order with the financial institution to perform the wire transfer.

Scope

3. SR VII applies, under the conditions set out below, to cross-border and domestic transfers between financial institutions.

Cross-border wire transfers

4. Cross-border wire transfers should be accompanied by accurate and meaningful originator information.[28]

5. Information accompanying cross-border wire transfers must always contain the name of the originator and where an account exists, the number of that account. In the absence of an account, a unique reference number must be included.

6. Information accompanying the wire transfer should also contain the address of the originator. However, jurisdictions may permit financial institutions to substitute the address with a national identity number, customer identification number, or date and place of birth.

---

[26] When this Interpretative Note was originally issued, these references were to the 1996 FATF Forty Recommendations. Subsequent to the publication of the revised FATF Forty Recommendations in June 2003, this text was updated accordingly. All references are now to the 2003 FATF Forty Recommendations.

[27] However, these systems do have a role in providing the necessary means for the financial institutions to fulfil their obligations under SR VII and, in particular, in preserving the integrity of the information transmitted with a wire transfer.

[28] Jurisdictions may have a de minimis threshold (no higher than USD 3,000) for a one-year period from publication of this Interpretative Note. At the end of this period, the FATF will undertake a review of this issue to determine whether the use of a de minimis threshold is acceptable. Notwithstanding any thresholds, accurate and meaningful originator information must be retained and made available by the ordering financing institution as set forth in paragraph 9.

7. Cross-border wire transfers that are contained within batch transfers, except for those sent by money remitters, will be treated as domestic wire transfers. In such cases, the ordering institutions must retain the information necessary to identify all originators and make it available on request to the authorities and to the beneficiary financial institution. Financial institutions should ensure that non-routine transactions are not batched where this would increase the risk of money laundering or terrorist financing.

Domestic wire transfers

8. Information accompanying domestic wire transfers must also include originator information as indicated for cross-border wire transfers, unless full originator information can be made available to the beneficiary financial institution and appropriate authorities by other means. In this latter case, financial institutions need only include the account number or a unique identifier provided that this number or identifier will permit the transaction to be traced back to the originator.

9. The information must be made available by the ordering financial institution within three business days of receiving the request either from the beneficiary financial institution or from appropriate authorities. Law enforcement authorities should be able to compel immediate production of such information.

Exemptions from SR VII

10. SR VII is not intended to cover the following types of payments:

   a. Any transfer that flows from a transaction carried out using a credit or debit card so long as the credit or debit card number accompanies all transfers flowing from the transaction. However, when credit or debit cards are used as a payment system to effect a money transfer, they are covered by SR VII, and the necessary information should be included in the message.

   b. Financial institution-to-financial institution transfers and settlements where both the originator person and the beneficiary person are financial institutions acting on their own behalf.

Role of ordering, intermediary and beneficiary financial institutions

Ordering financial institution

11. The ordering financial institution must ensure that qualifying wire transfers contain complete originator information. The ordering financial institution must also verify this information for accuracy and maintain this

information in accordance with the standards set out in the FATF Forty Recommendations (2003).[29]

Intermediary financial institution

12. For both cross-border and domestic wire transfers, financial institutions processing an intermediary element of such chains of wire transfers must ensure that all originator information that accompanies a wire transfer is retained with the transfer.

13. Where technical limitations prevent the full originator information accompanying a cross-border wire transfer from remaining with a related domestic wire transfer (during the necessary time to adapt payment systems), a record must be kept for five years by the receiving intermediary financial institution of all the information received from the ordering financial institution.

Beneficiary financial institution

14. Beneficiary financial institutions should have effective risk-based procedures in place to identify wire transfers lacking complete originator information. The lack of complete originator information may be considered as a factor in assessing whether a wire transfer or related transactions are suspicious and, as appropriate, whether they are thus required to be reported to the financial intelligence unit or other competent authorities. In some cases, the beneficiary financial institution should consider restricting or even terminating its business relationship with financial institutions that fail to meet SRVII standards.

Enforcement mechanisms for financial institutions that do not comply with wire transfer rules and regulations

15. Jurisdictions should adopt appropriate measures to monitor effectively the compliance of financial institutions with rules and regulations governing wire transfers. Financial institutions that fail to comply with such rules and regulations should be subject to civil, administrative or criminal sanctions.

---

[29] See footnote 2.

SPECIAL RECOMMENDATION VIII: NON-PROFIT ORGANISATIONS

COMBATING THE ABUSE OF NON-PROFIT ORGANISATIONS

INTERNATIONAL BEST PRACTICES

Introduction and definition

1. The misuse of non-profit organisations for the financing of terrorism is coming to be recognised as a crucial weak point in the global struggle to stop such funding at its source. This issue has captured the attention of the Financial Action Task Force (FATF), the G7, and the United Nations, as well as national authorities in many regions. Within the FATF, this has rightly become the priority focus of work to implement Special Recommendation VIII (Non-profit organisations).

2. Non-profit organisations can take on a variety of forms, depending on the jurisdiction and legal system. Within FATF members, law and practice recognise associations, foundations, fundraising committees, community service organisations, corporations of public interest, limited companies, Public Benevolent Institutions, all as legitimate forms of non-profit organisation, just to name a few.

3. This variety of legal forms, as well as the adoption of a risk-based approach to the problem, militates in favour of a functional, rather than a legalistic definition. Accordingly, the FATF has developed suggested practices that would best aid authorities to protect non-profit organisations **that engage in raising or disbursing funds** for charitable, religious, cultural, educational, social or fraternal purposes, or for the carrying out of other types of "good works" from being misused or exploited by the financiers of terrorism.

Statement of the Problem

4. Unfortunately, numerous instances have come to light in which the mechanism of charitable fundraising – *i.e.*, the collection of resources from donors and its redistribution for charitable purposes – has been used to provide a cover for the financing of terror. In certain cases, the organisation itself was a mere sham that existed simply to funnel money to terrorists. However, often the abuse of non-profit organisations occurred without the knowledge of donors, or even of members of the management and staff of the organisation itself, due to malfeasance by employees and/or managers diverting funding on their own. Besides financial support, some non-profit organisations have also provided cover and logistical support for the movement of terrorists and illicit arms. Some

examples of these kinds of activities were presented in the 2001-2002 FATF Report on Money Laundering Typologies;[30] others are presented in the annex to this paper.

Principles

5. The following principles guide the establishment of these best practices:

- The charitable sector is a vital component of the world economy and of many national economies and social systems that complements the activity of the governmental and business sectors in supplying a broad spectrum of public services and improving quality of life. We wish to safeguard and maintain the practice of charitable giving and the strong and diversified community of institutions through which it operates.

- Oversight of non-profit organisations is a co-operative undertaking among government, the charitable community, persons who support charity, and those whom it serves. Robust oversight mechanisms and a degree of institutional tension between non-profit organisations and government entities charged with their oversight do not preclude shared goals and complementary functions – both seek to promote transparency and accountability and, more broadly, common social welfare and security goals.

- Government oversight should be flexible, effective, and proportional to the risk of abuse. Mechanisms that reduce the compliance burden without creating loopholes for terrorist financiers should be given due consideration. Small organisations that do not raise significant amounts of money from public sources, and locally based associations or organisations whose primary function is to redistribute resources among members may not necessarily require enhanced government oversight.

- Different jurisdictions approach the regulation of non-profit organisations from different constitutional, legal, regulatory, and institutional frameworks, and any international standards or range of models must allow for such differences, while adhering to the goals of establishing transparency and accountability in the ways in which non-profit organisations collect and transmit funds. It is understood as well that jurisdictions may be restricted in their ability to regulate religious activity.

- Jurisdictions may differ on the scope of purposes and activities that are within the definition of "charity", but all should agree that it does not include activities that directly or indirectly support terrorism, including actions that could serve to induce or compensate for participation in terrorist acts.

---

[30] Published 1 February 2002 and available at http://www.fatf-gafi.org/FATDocs_en.htm#Trends.

- The non-profit sector in many jurisdictions has representational, self-regulatory, watchdog, and accreditation organisations that can and should play a role in the protection of the sector against abuse, in the context of a public-private partnership. Measures to strengthen self-regulation should be encouraged as a significant method of decreasing the risk of misuse by terrorist groups.

Areas of focus

6. Preliminary analysis of the investigations, blocking actions, and law-enforcement activities of various jurisdictions indicate several ways in which non-profit organisations have been misused by terrorists and suggests areas in which preventive measures should be considered.

i) Financial transparency

7. Non-profit organisations collect hundreds of billions of dollars annually from donors and distribute those monies – after paying for their own administrative costs – to beneficiaries. Transparency is in the interest of the donors, organisations, and authorities. However, the sheer volume of transactions conducted by non-profit organisations combined with the desire not to unduly burden legitimate organisations generally underscore the importance of risk and size-based proportionality in setting the appropriate level of rules and oversight in this area.

a. Financial accounting

- Non-profit organisations should maintain and be able to present full programme budgets that account for all programme expenses. These budgets should indicate the identity of recipients and how the money is to be used. The administrative budget should also be protected from diversion through similar oversight, reporting, and safeguards.

- Independent auditing is a widely recognised method of ensuring that accounts of an organisation accurately reflect the reality of its finances and should be considered a best practice. Many major non-profit organisations undergo audits to retain donor confidence, and regulatory authorities in some jurisdictions require them for non-profit organisations. Where practical, such audits should be conducted to ensure that such organisations are not being abused by terrorist groups. It should be noted that such financial auditing is not a guarantee that programme funds are actually reaching the intended beneficiaries.

b. Bank accounts

- It is considered a best practice for non-profit organisations that handle funds to maintain registered bank accounts, keep its funds in them, and utilise formal or registered financial channels for transferring funds, especially overseas. Where feasible, therefore, non-profit organisations that handle large amounts of money should use formal financial systems to conduct their financial transactions. Adoption of this best practice would bring the accounts of non-profit organisations, by and large, within the formal banking system and under the relevant controls or regulations of that system.

ii) Programmatic verification

8. The need to verify adequately the activities of a non-profit organisation is critical. In several instances, programmes that were reported to the home office were not being implemented as represented. The funds were in fact being diverted to terrorist organisations. Non-profit organisations should be in a position to know and to verify that funds have been spent as advertised and planned.

a. Solicitations

9. Solicitations for donations should accurately and transparently tell donors the purpose(s) for which donations are being collected. The non-profit organisation should then ensure that such funds are used for the purpose stated.

b. Oversight

10. To help ensure that funds are reaching the intended beneficiary, non-profit organisations should ask following general questions:

- Have projects actually been carried out?
- Are the beneficiaries real?
- Have the intended beneficiaries received the funds that were sent for them?
- Are all funds, assets, and premises accounted for?

c. Field examinations

11. In several instances, financial accounting and auditing might be insufficient protection against the abuse of non-profit organisations. Direct field audits of programmes may be, in some instances, the only method for detecting misdirection of funds. Examination of field operations is clearly a superior mechanism for discovering malfeasance of all kinds, including diversion of funds to terrorists. Given considerations of risk-based proportionality, across-the-board examination of all programmes would not be required. However, non-

profit organisations should track programme accomplishments as well as finances. Where warranted, examinations to verify reports should be conducted.

d. Foreign operations

12. When the home office of the non-profit organisation is in one country and the beneficent operations take place in another, the competent authorities of both jurisdictions should strive to exchange information and co-ordinate oversight or investigative work, in accordance with their comparative advantages. Where possible, a non-profit organisation should take appropriate measures to account for funds and services delivered in locations other than in its home jurisdiction.

iii) Administration

13. Non-profit organisations should be able to document their administrative, managerial, and policy control over their operations. The role of the Board of Directors, or its equivalent, is key.

14. Much has been written about the responsibilities of Boards of Directors in the corporate world and recent years have seen an increased focus and scrutiny of the important role of the Directors in the healthy and ethical functioning of the corporation. Directors of non-profit organisations, or those with equivalent responsibility for the direction and control of an organisation's management, likewise have a responsibility to act with due diligence and a concern that the organisation operates ethically. The directors or those exercising ultimate control over a non-profit organisation need to know who is acting in the organisation's name – in particular, responsible parties such as office directors, plenipotentiaries, those with signing authority and fiduciaries. Directors should exercise care, taking proactive verification measures whenever feasible, to ensure their partner organisations and those to which they provide funding, services, or material support, are not being penetrated or manipulated by terrorists.

15. Directors should act with diligence and probity in carrying out their duties. Lack of knowledge or passive involvement in the organisation's affairs does not absolve a director – or one who controls the activities or budget of a non-profit organisation – of responsibility. To this end, directors have responsibilities to:

- The organisation and its members to ensure the financial health of the organisation and that it focuses on its stated mandate.

- Those, with whom the organisation interacts, like donors, clients, suppliers.

- All levels of government that in any way regulate the organisation.

16. These responsibilities take on new meaning in light of the potential abuse of non-for-profit organisations for terrorist financing. If a non-profit organisation has a board of directors, the board of directors should:

- Be able to identify positively each board and executive member.
- Meet on a regular basis, keep records of the decisions taken at these meetings and through these meetings.
- Formalise the manner in which elections to the board are conducted as well as the manner in which a director can be removed.
- Ensure that there is an annual independent review of the finances and accounts of the organization.
- Ensure that there are appropriate financial controls over programme spending, including programs undertaken through agreements with other organizations.
- Ensure an appropriate balance between spending on direct programme delivery and administration.
- Ensure that procedures are put in place to prevent the use of the organisation's facilities or assets to support or condone terrorist activities.

Oversight bodies

17. Various bodies in different jurisdictions interact with the charitable community. In general, preventing misuse of non-profit organisations or fundraising organisations by terrorists has not been a historical focus of their work. Rather, the thrust of oversight, regulation, and accreditation to date has been maintaining donor confidence through combating waste and fraud, as well as ensuring that government tax relief benefits, where applicable, go to appropriate organisations. While much of this oversight focus is fairly easily transferable to the fight against terrorist finance, this will also require a broadening of focus.

18. There is not a single correct approach to ensuring appropriate transparency within non-profit organisations, and different jurisdictions use different methods to achieve this end. In some, independent charity commissions have an oversight role, in other jurisdictions government ministries are directly involved, just to take two examples. Tax authorities play a role in some jurisdictions, but not in others. Other authorities that have roles to play in the fight against terrorist finance include law enforcement agencies and bank regulators. Far from all the bodies are governmental – private sector watchdog or accreditation organisations play an important role in many jurisdictions.

i) Government Law Enforcement and Security officials

19. Non-profit organisations funding terrorism are operating illegally, just like any other illicit financier; therefore, much of the fight against the abuse of non-profit organisations will continue to rely heavily on law enforcement and security officials. Non-profit organisations are not exempt from the criminal laws that apply to individuals or business enterprises.

- Law enforcement and security officials should continue to play a key role in the combat against the abuse of non-profit organisations by terrorist groups, including by continuing their ongoing activities with regard to non-profit organisations.

ii) Specialised Government Regulatory Bodies

20. A brief overview of the pattern of specialised government regulation of non-profit organisations shows a great variety of practice. In England and Wales, such regulation is housed in a special Charities Commission. In the United States, any specialised government regulation occurs at the sub-national (state) level. GCC member countries oversee non-profit organisations with a variety of regulatory bodies, including government ministerial and intergovernmental agencies.

- In all cases, there should be interagency outreach and discussion within governments on the issue of terrorist financing – especially between those agencies that have traditionally dealt with terrorism and regulatory bodies that may not be aware of the terrorist financing risk to non-profit organisations. Specifically, terrorist financing experts should work with non-profit organisation oversight authorities to raise awareness of the problem, and they should alert these authorities to the specific characteristics of terrorist financing.

iii) Government Bank, Tax, and Financial Regulatory Authorities

21. While bank regulators are not usually engaged in the oversight of non-profit organisations, the earlier discussion of the importance of requiring charitable fund-raising and transfer of funds to go through formal or registered channels underscores the benefit of enlisting the established powers of the bank regulatory system – suspicious activity reporting, know-your-customer (KYC) rules, etc – in the fight against terrorist abuse or exploitation of non-profit organisations.

22. In those jurisdictions that provide tax benefits to charities, tax authorities have a high level of interaction with the charitable community. This expertise is of special importance to the fight against terrorist finance, since it tends to focus on the financial workings of charities.

- Jurisdictions which collect financial information on charities for the purposes of tax deductions should encourage the sharing of such information with government bodies involved in the combating of terrorism (including FIUs) to the maximum extent possible. Though such tax-related information may be sensitive, authorities should ensure that information relevant to the misuse of non-profit organisations by terrorist groups or supporters is shared as appropriate.

iv) Private Sector Watchdog Organisations

23. In the countries and jurisdictions where they exist, the private sector watchdog or accreditation organisations are a unique resource that should be a focal point of international efforts to combat the abuse of non-profit organisations by terrorists. Not only do they contain observers knowledgeable of fundraising organisations, they are also very directly interested in preserving the legitimacy and reputation of the non-profit organisations. More than any other class of participants, they have long been engaged in the development and promulgation of "best practices" for these organisations in a wide array of functions.

24. Jurisdictions should make every effort to reach out and engage such watchdog and accreditation organisations in their attempt to put best practices into place for combating the misuse of non-profit organisations. Such engagement could include a dialogue on how to improve such practices.

Sanctions

25. Countries should use existing laws and regulations or establish any such new laws or regulations to establish effective and proportionate administrative, civil, or criminal penalties for those who misuse charities for terrorist financing.

Typologies of Terrorist Misuse of Non-Profit Organisations

Example 1: Non-profit front organisation

1. In 1996, a number of individuals known to belong to the religious extremist groups established in the south-east of an FATF country (Country A) convinced wealthy foreign nationals, living for unspecified reasons in Country A, to finance the construction of a place of worship. These wealthy individuals were suspected of assisting in the concealment of part of the activities of a terrorist group. It was later established that "S", a businessman in the building sector, had bought the building intended to house the place of worship and had renovated it using funds from one of his companies. He then transferred the ownership of this building, for a large profit, to Group Y belonging to the wealthy foreigners mentioned above.

2. This place of worship intended for the local community in fact also served as a place to lodge clandestine "travellers" from extremist circles and collect funds. For example, soon after the work was completed, it was noticed that the place of worship was receiving large donations (millions of dollars) from other wealthy foreign businessmen. Moreover, a Group Y worker was said to have convinced his employers that a "foundation" would be more suitable for collecting and using large funds without attracting the attention of local authorities. A foundation was thus reportedly established for this purpose.

3. It is also believed that part of "S's" activities in heading a multipurpose international financial network (for which investments allegedly stood at USD 53 million for Country A in 1999 alone) was to provide support to a terrorist network. "S" had made a number of trips to Afghanistan and the United States. Amongst his assets were several companies registered in Country C and elsewhere. One of these companies, located in the capital of Country A, was allegedly a platform for collecting funds. "S" also purchased several buildings in the south of Country A with the potential collusion of a notary and a financial institution.

4. When the authorities of Country A blocked a property transaction on the basis of the foreign investment regulations, the financial institution's director stepped in to support his client's transaction and the notary presented a purchase document for the building thus ensuring that the relevant authorisation was delivered. The funds held by the bank were then transferred to another account in a bank in an NCCT jurisdiction to conceal their origin when they were used in Country A.

5. Even though a formal link has not as yet been established between the more or less legal activities of the parties in Country A and abroad and the financing of terrorist activities carried out under the authority a specific terrorist network, the investigators suspect that at least part of the proceeds from these activities have been used for this purpose.

Example 2: Fraudulent solicitation of donations

6. One non-profit organisation solicited donations from local charities in a donor region, in addition to fund raising efforts conducted at its headquarters in a beneficiary region. This non-profit organisation falsely asserted that the funds collected were destined for orphans and widows. In fact, the finance chief of this organisation served as the head of organised fundraising for Usama bin Laden. Rather than providing support for orphans and widows, funds collected by the non-profit organisation were turned over to al-Qaida operatives.

Example 3: Branch offices defraud headquarters

7. The office director for a non-profit organisation in a beneficiary region defrauded donors from a donor region to fund terrorism. In order to obtain additional funds from the headquarters, the branch office padded the number of orphans it claimed to care for by providing names of orphans that did not exist or who had died. Funds then sent for the purpose of caring for the non-existent or dead orphans were instead diverted to al-Qaida terrorists.

8. In addition, the branch office in a beneficiary region of another non-profit organisation based in a donor region provided a means of funnelling money to a known local terrorist organisation by disguising funds as intended to be used for orphanage projects or the construction of schools and houses of worship. The office also employed members of the terrorist organisations and facilitated their travel.

Example 4: Aid worker's Misuse of Position

9. An employee working for an aid organisation in a war-ravaged region used his employment to support the ongoing activities of a known terrorist organisation from another region. While working for the aid organisation as a monitor for work funded in that region, the employee secretly made contact with weapons smugglers in the region. He used his position as cover as he brokered the purchase and export of weapons to the terrorist organisation.

Guidance for Financial Institutions in Detecting Terrorist Financing

Introduction

1. At its extraordinary Plenary meeting on 29-30 October 2001, the Financial Action Task Force on Money Laundering (FATF) agreed to develop special guidance for financial institutions to help them detect the techniques and mechanisms used in the financing of terrorism. The FATF subsequently brought together experts from its member countries to gather information on and study the issue of terrorist financing as part of its annual exercise on money laundering methods and trends. One goal of this exercise was to begin establishing such guidance for financial institutions that could be issued along with the annual FATF Report on Money Laundering Methods and Trends. Material derived from the exercise, along with contributions from the Egmont Group and other international bodies, was used in developing the present document. The information contained in it represents a first attempt to provide necessary guidance for financial institutions in this area.

2. The goal in providing this guidance is to ensure that financial institutions do not unwittingly hide or move terrorist funds. Financial institutions will thus be better able to protect themselves from being used as a conduit for such activity. To help build awareness of how terrorists, their associates or those who support terrorism may use the financial system, this document describes the general characteristics of terrorist financing. The accompanying case studies illustrate the manner in which competent law enforcement authorities or financial intelligence units (FIUs) are able to establish a terrorist financing link based on information reported by financial institutions. Annex 1 contains a series of characteristics of financial transactions that have been linked to terrorist activity in the past. When one or several of these potentially suspicious or unusual factors is present in regard to a specific financial transaction – especially when the individual or entity may appear on one of the lists of suspected terrorists, terrorist organisations or associated individuals and entities (see Annex 2: Sources of Information) – then a financial institution would have cause to increase its scrutiny of the transaction and any associated individuals or entities. In certain instances, this scrutiny could result in reporting the transaction to authorities under applicable suspicious or unusual transaction reporting systems.

THE FINANCIAL WAR ON TERRORISM – ISBN 92-64-10610-3 – FATF-GAFI 2004

Terrorist financing and risks to financial institutions

3. A financial institution that carries out a transaction, knowing that the funds or property involved are owned or controlled by terrorists or terrorist organisations, or that the transaction is linked to, or likely to be used in, terrorist activity, may be committing a criminal offence under the laws of many jurisdictions. Such an offence may exist regardless of whether the assets involved in the transaction were the proceeds of criminal activity or were derived from lawful activity but intended for use in support of terrorism.

4. Regardless of whether the funds in a transaction are related to terrorists for the purposes of national criminal legislation, business relationships with such individuals or other closely associated persons or entities could, under certain circumstances, expose a financial institution to significant reputational, operational, and legal risk. This risk is even more serious if the person or entity involved is later shown to have benefited from the lack of effective monitoring or wilful blindness of a particular institution and thus was to carry out terrorist acts.

Reinforcing existing requirements

5. Consideration of the factors contained in this guidance is intended to clarify, complement and/or reinforce already existing due diligence requirements, along with current policies and procedures imposed by national anti-money laundering programmes. It should be stressed, however, that this guidance does not constitute an additional rule or regulation. Rather it represents advice from the operational experts of FATF members as to factors associated with financial transactions that should trigger further questions on the part of the financial institution. The FATF encourages all financial institutions to consider these factors along with policies, practices and procedures already in place for ensuring compliance with appropriate laws and regulations and for minimising reputational risks. It should be noted as well that, while the characteristics indicated in this document may apply specifically to terrorist financing, most of them may also apply in identifying suspicious transactions generally. Financial institutions in many jurisdictions may already be aware of these characteristics through existing guidance notes or other sources.

6. In providing this guidance, the FATF intends it to be consistent with applicable criminal and civil laws, as well as relevant regulations, to which financial institutions may be subject in their particular jurisdiction. It should be noted however that this guidance does not replace or supersede any obligations under the current national laws or regulations. In particular, implementing the measures proposed by this guidance should not be construed as necessarily protecting a financial institution from any action that a jurisdiction might

choose to take against it. Furthermore, this guidance does not supersede or modify requirements imposed by national or regional authorities, which call for the freezing of assets of individuals and entities suspected of being terrorists or terrorist related, as part of implementing relevant United Nations Security Council Resolutions (see Annex 2: Sources of Information).

Determining when increased scrutiny is necessary

7. Financial institutions are encouraged to develop practices and procedures that will help to detect and deter those transactions that may involve funds used in terrorist financing. The increased scrutiny that may be warranted for some transactions should be seen as a further application of the institution's due diligence and anti-money laundering policies and procedures and should lead, when appropriate, to reporting of such financial activity as suspicious or unusual under applicable transaction reporting regimes for a particular jurisdiction. To ensure that the practical steps are taken to increase scrutiny of certain transactions when necessary, it may be useful for a financial institution to review its practices in this area as part of its general internal and external audit processes.

8. The manner in which a financial institution may choose to apply this Guidance will vary depending on the extent of the risk determined to exist by each institution as a general matter, given its normal business operations. It will also vary according to the individual factors of each case as it occurs. Financial institutions should exercise reasonable judgement in modifying and implementing policies and procedures in this area. This Guidance should not be interpreted as discouraging or prohibiting financial institutions from doing business with any legitimate customer. Indeed, it has been designed solely as a means of assisting financial institutions in determining whether a transaction merits additional scrutiny so that the institution is thus better able to identify, report (when appropriate) and ultimately avoid transactions involving the funds supporting or associated with the financing of terrorism.

9. It should be acknowledged as well that financial institutions will probably be unable to detect terrorist financing as such. Indeed, the only time that financial institutions might clearly identify terrorist financing as distinct from other criminal misuse of the financial system is when a known terrorist or terrorist organisation has opened an account. Financial institutions are, however, in a position to detect suspicious transactions that, if reported, may later prove to be related to terrorist financing. It is the competent enforcement authority or the financial intelligence unit (FIU) then that is in a position to determine whether the transaction relates to a particular type of criminal or

Example 1: *Front for individual with suspected terrorist links revealed by suspicious transaction report*

The financial intelligence unit (FIU) in Country D received a suspicious transaction report from a domestic financial institution regarding an account held by an individual residing in a neighbouring country. The individual managed European-based companies and had filed two loan applications on their behalf with the reporting institution. These loan applications amounted to several million US dollars and were ostensibly intended for the purchase of luxury hotels in Country D. The bank did not grant any of the loans.

The analysis by the FIU revealed that the funds for the purchase of the hotels were to be channelled through the accounts of the companies represented by the individual. One of the companies making the purchase of these hotels would then have been taken over by an individual from another country. This second person represented a group of companies whose activities focused on hotel and leisure sectors, and he appeared to be the ultimate buyer of the real estate. On the basis of the analysis within the FIU, it appeared that the subject of the suspicious transaction report was acting as a front for the second person. The latter as well as his family are suspected of being linked to terrorism.

terrorist activity and decide on a course of action. For this reason, financial institutions do not necessarily need to determine the legality of the source or destination of the funds. Instead, they should ascertain whether transactions are unusual, suspicious or otherwise indicative of criminal or terrorist activity.

Characteristics of terrorist financing

10. The primary objective of terrorism according to one definition is "to intimidate a population, or to compel a Government of an international organisation to do or abstain from doing any act".[31] In contrast, financial gain is generally the objective of other types of criminal activities. While the difference in ultimate goals between each of these activities may be true to some extent, terrorist organisations still require financial support in order to achieve their aims. A successful terrorist group, like any criminal organisation, is therefore necessarily one that is able to build and maintain an effective financial infrastructure. For this it must develop sources of funding, a means of laundering those funds and then finally a way to ensure that the funds can be used to obtain material and other logistical items needed to commit terrorist acts.

Sources of terrorist funds

11. Experts generally believe that terrorist financing comes from two primary sources. The first source is the financial support provided by States or organisations with large enough infrastructures to collect and then make funds available to the terrorist organisation. This so-called State-sponsored terrorism has declined in recent years, according to some experts, and is increasingly replaced by other types of backing. An individual with sufficient financial means may also provide substantial funding to terrorist groups. Osama bin Laden, for example, is thought to have contributed significant amounts of his personal fortune to the establishment and support of the Al-Qaida terrorist network.

12. The second major source of funds for terrorist organisations is income derived directly from various "revenue-generating" activities. As with criminal organisations, a terrorist group's income may be derived from crime or other unlawful activities. A terrorist group in a particular region may support itself through kidnapping and extortion. In this scenario, ransoms paid to retrieve hostages, along with a special "revolutionary tax" (in reality a euphemism for protection money) demanded of businesses, provide needed financial resources but also play a secondary role as one other means of intimidating the target population. Besides kidnapping and extortion, terrorist groups may engage in

---

[31] Art. 2, *International Convention for the Suppression of the Financing of Terrorism*, 9 December 1999.

Example 2: *Individual's account activity and inclusion on UN list show possible link to terrorist activity*

An individual resided in a neighbouring country but had a demand deposit account and a savings account in Country N. The bank that maintained the accounts noticed the gradual withdrawal of funds from the accounts from the end of April 2001 onwards and decided to monitor the accounts more closely. The suspicions of the bank were subsequently reinforced when a name very similar to the account holder's appeared in the consolidated list of persons and/of entities issued by the United Nations Security Council Committee on Afghanistan (UN Security Council Resolution 1333/2000). The bank immediately made a report to the financial intelligence unit (FIU).

The FIU analysed the financial movements relating to the individual's accounts using records requested from the bank. It appeared that both of the accounts had been opened by the individual in 1990 and had been fed mostly by cash deposits. In March 2000 the individual made a sizeable transfer from his savings account to his checking account. These funds were used to pay for a single premium life insurance policy and to purchase certificates of deposit.

From the middle of April 2001 the individual made several large transfers from his savings account to his demand deposit account. These funds were transferred abroad to persons and companies located in neighbouring countries and in other regions.

In May and June 2001, the individual sold the certificates of deposit he had purchased, and he then transferred the profits to the accounts of companies based in Asia and to that of a company established in his country of origin. The individual also cashed in his life insurance policy before the maturity date and transferred its value to an account at a bank in his country of origin. The last transaction was carried out on 30 August 2001, that is, shortly before the September 11th attacks in the United States.

Finally, the anti-money laundering unit in the individual's county of origin communicated information related to suspicious operations carried out by him and by the companies that received the transfers. Many of these names also appeared in the files of the FIU. This case is currently under investigation.

Large-scale smuggling, various types of fraud (for example, through credit cards or charities), thefts and robbery, and narcotics trafficking.

13. Funding for terrorist groups, unlike for criminal organisations however, may also include income derived from legitimate sources or from a combination of lawful and unlawful sources. Indeed, this funding from legal sources is a key difference between terrorist groups and traditional criminal organisations. How much of a role that legal money plays in the support of terrorism varies according to the terrorist group and whether the source of funds is in the same geographic location as the terrorist acts the group commits.

14. Community solicitation and fundraising appeals are one very effective means of raising funds to support terrorism. Often such fundraising is carried out in the name of organisations having the status of a charitable or relief organisation, and it may be targeted at a particular community. Some members of the community are led to believe that they are giving for a good cause. In many cases, the charities to which donations are given are in fact legitimate in that they do engage in some of the work they purport to carry out. Most of the members of the organisation, however, have no knowledge that a portion of the funds raised by the charity is being diverted to terrorist causes. For example, the supporters of a terrorist movement from one country may carry out ostensibly legal activities in another country to obtain financial resources. The movement's supporters raise these funds by infiltrating and taking control of institutions within the immigrant community of the second country. Some of the specific fundraising methods might include: collection of membership dues and/or subscriptions; sale of publications; speaking tours, cultural and social events; door-to-door solicitation within the community; appeals to wealthy members of the community; and donations of a portion of their personal earnings.

Laundering of terrorist related funds

15. From a technical perspective, the methods used by terrorists and their associates to generate funds from illegal sources differ little from those used by traditional criminal organisations. Although it would seem logical that funding from legitimate sources would not need to be laundered, there is nevertheless often a need for the terrorist group to obscure or disguise links between it and its legitimate funding sources. It follows then that terrorist groups must similarly find ways to launder these funds in order to be able to use them without drawing the attention of authorities. In examining terrorist related financial activity, FATF experts have concluded that terrorists and their support organisations generally use the same methods as criminal groups to launder funds. Some of the particular methods detected with respect to various terrorist groups include: cash smuggling (both by couriers or bulk cash shipments), structured deposits to or withdrawals from bank accounts, purchases of various types of monetary instruments (travellers' cheques, bank cheques, money orders), use of credit or debit cards, and wire

Example 3: *Diamond trading company possibly linked to terrorist funding operation*

The financial intelligence unit (FIU) in Country C received several suspicious transaction reports from different banks concerning two persons and a diamond trading company. The individuals and the company in question were account holders at the various banks. In the space of a few months, a large number of fund transfers to and from overseas were made from the accounts of the two individuals. Moreover, soon after the account was opened, one of the individuals received several USD cheques for large amounts.

According to information obtained by the FIU, one of the accounts held by the company appeared to have received large US dollar deposit originating from companies active in the diamond industry. One of the directors of the company, a citizen of Country C but residing in Africa, maintained an account at another bank in Country C. Several transfers had been carried out to and from overseas using this account. The transfers from foreign countries were mainly in US dollars. They were converted into the local currency and were then transferred to foreign countries and to accounts in the Country C belonging to one of the two subjects of the suspicious transaction report.

Police information obtained by the FIU revealed that an investigation had already been initiated relating to these individuals and the trafficking of diamonds originating from Africa. The large funds transfers by the diamond trading company were mainly sent to the same person residing in another region. Police sources revealed that this person and the individual that had cashed the cheques were suspected of buying diamonds from the rebel army of an African country and then smuggling them into Country C on behalf of a terrorist organisation. Further research by the FIU also revealed links between the subjects of the suspicious transaction report and individuals and companies already tied to the laundering of funds for organised crime. This case is currently under investigation.

transfers. There have also been indications that some forms of underground banking (particularly the hawala system[32]) have had a role in moving terrorist related funds.

16. The difference between legally and illegally obtained proceeds raises an important legal problem as far as applying anti-money laundering measures to terrorist financing. Money laundering has generally been defined as a process whereby funds obtained through or generated by criminal activity are moved or concealed in order to obscure the link between the crime and generated funds. The terrorist's ultimate aim on the other hand is not to generate profit from his fundraising mechanisms but to obtain resources to support his operations. In a number of countries, terrorist financing thus may not yet be included as a predicate offence for money laundering, and it may be impossible therefore to apply preventive and repressive measures specifically targeting this terrorist activity.

17. When terrorists or terrorist organisations obtain their financial support from legal sources (donations, sales of publications, etc.), there are certain factors that make detecting and tracing these funds more difficult. For example, charities or non-profit organisations and other legal entities have been cited as playing an important role in the financing of some terrorist groups. The apparent legal source of this funding may mean that there are few, if any, indicators that would make an individual financial transaction or series of transactions stand out as linked to terrorist activities.

18. Other important aspects of terrorist financing that make its detection more difficult are the size and nature of the transactions involved. Several FATF experts have mentioned that the funding needed to mount a terrorist attack does not always call for large sums of money, and the associated transactions are usually not complex. For example, an examination of the financial connections among the September 11th hijackers showed that most of the individual transactions were small sums, that is, below the usual cash transaction reporting thresholds, and in most cases the operations consisted of only wire transfers. The individuals were ostensibly foreign students who appeared to be receiving money from their parents or in the form of grants for their studies, thus the transactions would not have been identified as needing additional scrutiny by the financial institutions involved.

---

[32] For more information on the hawala system of alternate remittance / underground banking, see the 1999-2000 FATF Report on Money Laundering Typologies, 3 February 2001 (pp. 4-8).

Example 4: *Cash deposits to accounts of non-profit organisation allegedly finance terrorist group.*

The financial intelligence unit (FIU) in Country L received a suspicious transaction report from a bank regarding an account held by an offshore investment company. The bank's suspicions arose after the company's manager made several large cash deposits in different foreign currencies. According to the customer, these funds were intended to finance companies in the media sector. The FIU requested information from several financial institutions. Through these enquiries, it learned that the managers of the offshore investment company were residing in Country L and a bordering country. They had opened accounts at various banks in Country L under the names of media companies and a non-profit organisation involved in the promotion of cultural activities. According to the analysis by the FIU, the managers of the offshore investment company and several other clients had made cash deposits to the accounts. These funds were ostensibly intended for the financing of media based projects. The analysis further revealed that the account held by the non-profit organisation was receiving almost daily deposits in small amounts by third parties. The manager of this organisation stated that the money deposited in this account was coming from its members for the funding of cultural activities.

Police information obtained by the FIU revealed that the managers of offshore investment company were known to have been involved in money laundering and that an investigation was already underway into their activities. The managers appeared to be members of a terrorist group, which was financed by extortion and narcotics trafficking. Funds were collected through the non-profit organisation from the different suspects involved in this case. This case is currently under investigation.

Example 5: *High account turnover indicates fraud allegedly used to finance terrorist organisation*

An investigation in Country B arose as a consequence of a suspicious transaction report. A financial institution reported that an individual who allegedly earned a salary of just over USD 17 000 per annum had a turnover in his account of nearly USD 356 000. Investigators subsequently learned that this individual did not exist and that the account had been fraudulently obtained. Further investigation revealed that the account was linked to a foreign charity and was used to facilitate funds collection for a terrorist organisation through a fraud scheme. In Country B, the government provides matching funds to charities in an amount equivalent to 42 per cent of donations received. Donations to this charity were being paid into to the account under investigation, and the government matching funds were being claimed by the charity. The original donations were then returned to the donors so that effectively no donation had been given to the charity. The charity retained the matching funds. This fraud resulted in over USD 1.14 million being fraudulently obtained. This case is currently under investigation.

ANNEX 1: CHARACTERISTICS OF FINANCIAL TRANSACTIONS THAT MAY BE A CAUSE FOR INCREASED SCRUTINY

As a normal part of carrying out their work, financial institutions should be aware of elements of individual transactions that could indicate funds involved in terrorist financing. The following list of potentially suspicious or unusual activities is meant to show types of transactions that could be a cause for additional scrutiny. This list is not exhaustive, nor does it take the place of any legal obligations related to the reporting suspicious or unusual transactions that may be imposed by individual national authorities.

This list of characteristics should be taken into account by financial institutions along with other available information (including any lists of suspected terrorists, terrorist groups, and associated individuals and entities issued by the United Nations[33] or appropriate national authorities – see Annex 2 : Sources of Information), the nature of the transaction itself, and the parties involved in the transaction, as well as any other guidance that may be provided by national anti-money laundering authorities. The existence of one or more of the factors described in this list may warrant some form of increased scrutiny of the transaction. However, the existence of one of these factors by itself does not necessarily mean that a transaction is suspicious or unusual. For examples of terrorist financing cases developed from the enhanced scrutiny/reporting by financial institutions, please also see the various case examples provided in the body of the main document.

Financial institutions should pay particular attention to:

A. Accounts

1) Accounts that receive relevant periodical deposits and are dormant at other periods. These accounts are then used in creating a legitimate appearing financial background through which additional fraudulent activities may be carried out.

2) A dormant account containing a minimal sum suddenly receives a deposit or series of deposits followed by daily cash withdrawals that continue until the transferred sum has been removed.

---

[33] This guidance does not supersede or modify requirements imposed by national or regional authorities, which call for the freezing of assets of individuals and entities suspected of being terrorists or terrorist related, as part of implementing relevant United Nations Security Council Resolutions.

Example 6: *Lack of clear business relationship appears to point terrorist connection*

The manager of a chocolate factory (CHOCCo) introduced the manager of his bank accounts to two individuals, both company managers, who were interested in opening commercial bank accounts. The two companies were established within a few days of each other, however in different countries. The first company (TEXTCo) was involved in the textile trade while the second one was a real estate (REALCo) non-trading company. The companies had different managers and their activities were not connected.

The bank manager opened the accounts for the two companies, which thereafter remained dormant. After several years, the manager of the chocolate factory announced the arrival of a credit transfer issued by the REALCo to the account of the TEXTCo. This transfer was ostensibly an advance on an order of tablecloths. No invoice was shown. However, once the account of TEXTCo received the funds, its manager asked for them to be made available in cash at a bank branch near the border. There, accompanied by the manager of CHOCCo, the TEXTCo manager withdrew the cash.

The bank reported this information to the financial intelligence unit (FIU). The FIU's research showed that the two men crossed the border with the money after making the cash withdrawal. The border region is one in which terrorist activity occurs, and further information from the intelligence services indicated links between the managers of TEXTCo and REALCo and terrorist organisations active in that region.

3) When opening an account, the customer refuses to provide information required by the financial institution, attempts to reduce the level of information provided to the minimum or provides information that is misleading or difficult to verify.

4) An account for which several persons have signature authority, yet these persons appear to have no relation among each other (either family ties or business relationship).

5) An account opened by a legal entity or an organisation that has the same address as other legal entities or organisations but for which the same person or persons have signature authority, when there is no apparent economic or legal reason for such an arrangement (for example, individuals serving as company directors for multiple companies headquartered at the same location, etc.).

6) An account opened in the name of a recently formed legal entity and in which a higher than expected level of deposits are made in comparison with the income of the founders of the entity.

7) The opening by the same person of multiple accounts into which numerous small deposits are made that in aggregate are not commensurate with the expected income of the customer.

8) An account opened in the name of a legal entity that is involved in the activities of an association or foundation whose aims are related to the claims or demands of a terrorist organisation.

9) An account opened in the name of a legal entity, a foundation or an association, which may be linked to a terrorist organisation and that shows movements of funds above the expected level of income.

B. Deposits and withdrawals

1) Deposits for a business entity in combinations of monetary instruments that are atypical of the activity normally associated with such a business (for example, deposits that include a mix of business, payroll and social security cheques).

2) Large cash withdrawals made from a business account not normally associated with cash transactions.

3) Large cash deposits made to the account of an individual or legal entity when the apparent business activity of the individual or entity would normally be conducted in cheques or other payment instruments.

4) Mixing of cash deposits and monetary instruments in an account in which such transactions do not appear to have any relation to the normal use of the account.

5) Multiple transactions carried out on the same day at the same branch of a financial institution but with an apparent attempt to use different tellers.

6) The structuring of deposits through multiple branches of the same financial institution or by groups of individuals who enter a single branch at the same time.

7) The deposit or withdrawal of cash in amounts which fall consistently just below identification or reporting thresholds.

8) The presentation of uncounted funds for a transaction. Upon counting, the transaction is reduced to an amount just below that which would trigger reporting or identification requirements.

9) The deposit or withdrawal of multiple monetary instruments at amounts which fall consistently just below identification or reporting thresholds, particularly if the instruments are sequentially numbered.

C. Wire transfers

1) Wire transfers ordered in small amounts in an apparent effort to avoid triggering identification or reporting requirements.

2) Wire transfers to or for an individual where information on the originator, or the person on whose behalf the transaction is conducted, is not provided with the wire transfer, when the inclusion of such information would be expected.

3) Use of multiple personal and business accounts or the accounts of non-profit organisations or charities to collect and then funnel funds immediately or after a short time to a small number of foreign beneficiaries.

4) Foreign exchange transactions that are performed on behalf of a customer by a third party followed by wire transfers of the funds to locations having no apparent business connection with the customer or to countries of specific concern.

D. Characteristics of the customer or his/her business activity

1) Funds generated by a business owned by individuals of the same origin or involvement of multiple individuals of the same origin from countries of specific concern acting on behalf of similar business types.

2) Shared address for individuals involved in cash transactions, particularly when the address is also a business location and/or does not seem to correspond to the stated occupation (for example student, unemployed, self-employed, etc.).

3) Stated occupation of the transactor is not commensurate with the level or type of activity (for example, a student or an unemployed individual who

receives or sends large numbers of wire transfers, or who makes daily maximum cash withdrawals at multiple locations over a wide geographic area).

4) Regarding non-profit or charitable organisations, financial transactions for which there appears to be no logical economic purpose or in which there appears to be no link between the stated activity of the organisation and the other parties in the transaction.

5) A safe deposit box is opened on behalf of a commercial entity when the business activity of the customer is unknown or such activity does not appear to justify the use of a safe deposit box.

6) Unexplained inconsistencies arising from the process of identifying or verifying the customer (for example, regarding previous or current country of residence, country of issue of the passport, countries visited according to the passport, and documents furnished to confirm name, address and date of birth).

E. Transactions linked to locations of concern

1) Transactions involving foreign currency exchanges that are followed within a short time by wire transfers to locations of specific concern (for example, countries designated by national authorities, FATF non-co-operative countries and territories, etc.).

2) Deposits are followed within a short time by wire transfers of funds, particularly to or through a location of specific concern (for example, countries designated by national authorities, FATF non-co-operative countries and territories, etc.).

3) A business account through which a large number of incoming or outgoing wire transfers take place and for which there appears to be no logical business or other economic purpose, particularly when this activity is to, through or from locations of specific concern.

4) The use of multiple accounts to collect and then funnel funds to a small number of foreign beneficiaries, both individuals and businesses, particularly when these are in locations of specific concern.

5) A customer obtains a credit instrument or engages in commercial financial transactions involving movement of funds to or from locations of specific concern when there appears to be no logical business reasons for dealing with those locations.

6) The opening of accounts of financial institutions from locations of specific concern.

7) Sending or receiving funds by international transfers from and/or to locations of specific concern.

ANNEX 2: SOURCES OF INFORMATION

Several sources of information exist that may help financial institutions in determining whether a potentially suspicious or unusual transaction could indicate funds involved in the financing of terrorism and thus be subject to reporting obligations under national anti-money laundering or antiterrorism laws and regulations.

A. United Nations list
Committee on S/RES/1267 (1999)
website: *http://www.un.org/Docs/sc/committees/AfghanTemplate.htm*

B. Other lists

1) Financial Action Task Force
FATF Identification of Non-Co-operative Countries and Territories
 website: *http://www.fatf-gafi.org/NCCT_en.htm*

2) United States
Executive Order 13224, 23 September 2001 (with updates)
US Department of the Treasury website: *http://www.ustreas.gov/terrorism.html*

3) Council of the European Union
Council Regulation (EC) N° 467/2001 of 6 March 2001 [on freezing Taliban funds]
Council Decision (EC) N° 927/2001 of 27 December 2001 [list of terrorists and terrorist organisations whose assets should be frozen in accordance with Council Regulation (EC) N° 2580/2001]
Council Common Position of 27 December 2001 on application of specific measures to combat terrorism [list of persons, groups and entities involved in terrorist acts]
EUR-lex website: *http://europa.eu.int/eur-lex/en/index.html*

C. Standards

1) Financial Action Task Force
FATF Special Recommendations on Terrorist Financing
FATF website: *http://www.fatf-gafi.org/TerFinance_en.htm*
FATF Forty Recommendations on Money Laundering
FATF website: *http://www.fatf-gafi.org/40Recs_en.htm*

2) UN Conventions and Resolutions
International Convention on the Suppression of Terrorist Financing
Website: *http://untreaty.un.org/English/Terrorism.asp*
UN Security Council Resolutions on Terrorism
Website: *http://www.un.org/terrorism/sc.htm*

3) Council of the European Union
Council Regulation (EC) N° 2580/2001 of 27 December 2001 on specific restrictive measures directed against certain persons and entities with a view to combating terrorism
EUR-lex website: *http://europa.eu.int/eur-lex/en/index.html*

PART 2: MONEY LAUNDERING

The FATF Forty Recommendations	p. 91
Glossary	p. 111
Interpretative Notes	p. 115

THE FATF FORTY RECOMMENDATIONS

INTRODUCTION

Money laundering methods and techniques change in response to developing counter-measures. In recent years, the Financial Action Task Force (FATF) has noted increasingly sophisticated combinations of techniques, such as the increased use of legal persons to disguise the true ownership and control of illegal proceeds, and an increased use of professionals to provide advice and assistance in laundering criminal funds. These factors, combined with the experience gained through the FATF's Non-Co-operative Countries and Territories process, and a number of national and international initiatives, led the FATF to review and revise the Forty Recommendations into a new comprehensive framework for combating money laundering and terrorist financing. The FATF now calls upon all countries to take the necessary steps to bring their national systems for combating money laundering and terrorist financing into compliance with the new FATF Recommendations, and to effectively implement these measures.

The review process for revising the Forty Recommendations was an extensive one, open to FATF members, non-members, observers, financial and other affected sectors and interested parties. This consultation process provided a wide range of input, all of which was considered in the review process.

The revised Forty Recommendations now apply not only to money laundering but also to terrorist financing, and when combined with the Eight Special Recommendations on Terrorist Financing provide an enhanced, comprehensive and consistent framework of measures for combating money laundering and terrorist financing. The FATF recognises that countries have diverse legal and financial systems and so all cannot take identical measures to achieve the common objective, especially over matters of detail. The Recommendations therefore set minimum standards for action for countries to implement the detail according to their particular circumstances and constitutional frameworks. The Recommendations cover all the measures that national systems should have in place within their criminal justice and regulatory systems; the preventive measures to be taken by financial institutions and certain other businesses and professions; and international co-operation.

The original FATF Forty Recommendations were drawn up in 1990 as an initiative to combat the misuse of financial systems by persons laundering drug money. In 1996 the Recommendations were revised for the first time to reflect evolving money laundering typologies. The 1996 Forty Recommendations have been endorsed by more than 130 countries and are the international anti-money laundering standard.

In October 2001 the FATF expanded its mandate to deal with the issue of the financing of terrorism, and took the important step of creating the Eight Special Recommendations on Terrorist Financing.

These Recommendations contain a set of measures aimed at combating the funding of terrorist acts and terrorist organisations, and are complementary to the Forty Recommendations.[34]

A key element in the fight against money laundering and the financing of terrorism is the need for countries' systems to be monitored and evaluated, with respect to these international standards. The mutual evaluations conducted by the FATF and FATF-style regional bodies, as well as the assessments conducted by the IMF and World Bank, are a vital mechanism for ensuring that the FATF Recommendations are effectively implemented by all countries.

---

[34] The FATF Forty and Eight Special Recommendations have been recognised by the International Monetary Fund and the World Bank as the international standards for combating money laundering and the financing of terrorism.

THE FORTY RECOMMENDATIONS *

A. LEGAL SYSTEMS

Scope of the criminal offence of money laundering

1. Countries should criminalise money laundering on the basis of the 1988 United Nations Convention against Illicit Traffic in Narcotic Drugs and Psychotropic Substances (the Vienna Convention) and the 2000 United Nations Convention on Transnational Organized Crime (the Palermo Convention).

   Countries should apply the crime of money laundering to all serious offences, with a view to including the widest range of predicate offences. Predicate offences may be described by reference to all offences, or to a threshold linked either to a category of serious offences or to the penalty of imprisonment applicable to the predicate offence (threshold approach), or to a list of predicate offences, or a combination of these approaches.

   Where countries apply a threshold approach, predicate offences should at a minimum comprise all offences that fall within the category of serious offences under their national law or should include offences which are punishable by a maximum penalty of more than one year's imprisonment or for those countries that have a minimum threshold for offences in their legal system, predicate offences should comprise all offences, which are punished by a minimum penalty of more than six months imprisonment.

   Whichever approach is adopted, each country should at a minimum include a range of offences within each of the designated categories of offences (see Glossary).

   Predicate offences for money laundering should extend to conduct that occurred in another country, which constitutes an offence in that country and which would have constituted a predicate offence had it occurred domestically. Countries may provide that the only prerequisite is that the conduct would have constituted a predicate offence had it occurred domestically.

---

* Recommendations marked with an asterisk should be read in conjunction with their Interpretative Note.

Countries may provide that the offence of money laundering does not apply to persons who committed the predicate offence, where this is required by fundamental principles of their domestic law.

2. Countries should ensure that:

a) The intent and knowledge required to prove the offence of money laundering is consistent with the standards set forth in the Vienna and Palermo Conventions, including the concept that such mental state may be inferred from objective factual circumstances.

b) Criminal liability, and, where that is not possible, civil or administrative liability, should apply to legal persons. This should not preclude parallel criminal, civil or administrative proceedings with respect to legal persons in countries in which such forms of liability are available. Legal persons should be subject to effective, proportionate and dissuasive sanctions. Such measures should be without prejudice to the criminal liability of individuals.

Provisional measures and confiscation

3. Countries should adopt measures similar to those set forth in the Vienna and Palermo Conventions, including legislative measures, to enable their competent authorities to confiscate property laundered, proceeds from money laundering or predicate offences, instrumentalities used in or intended for use in the commission of these offences, or property of corresponding value, without prejudicing the rights of bona fide third parties.

Such measures should include the authority to: *a)* identify, trace and evaluate property which is subject to confiscation; *b)* carry out provisional measures, such as freezing and seizing, to prevent any dealing, transfer or disposal of such property; *c)* take steps that will prevent or void actions that prejudice the State's ability to recover property that is subject to confiscation; and *d)* take any appropriate investigative measures.

Countries may consider adopting measures that allow such proceeds or instrumentalities to be confiscated without requiring a criminal conviction, or which require an offender to demonstrate the lawful origin of the property alleged to be liable to confiscation, to the extent that such a requirement is consistent with the principles of their domestic law.

B. MEASURES TO BE TAKEN BY FINANCIAL INSTITUTIONS AND NONFINANCIAL BUSINESSES AND PROFESSIONS TO PREVENT MONEY LAUNDERING AND TERRORIST FINANCING

4. Countries should ensure that financial institution secrecy laws do not inhibit implementation of the FATF Recommendations.

Customer due diligence and record-keeping

5.* Financial institutions should not keep anonymous accounts or accounts in obviously fictitious names.

Financial institutions should undertake customer due diligence measures, including identifying and verifying the identity of their customers, when:

- establishing business relations;

- carrying out occasional transactions: *i)* above the applicable designated threshold; or *ii)*that are wire transfers in the circumstances covered by the Interpretative Note to Special Recommendation VII;

- there is a suspicion of money laundering or terrorist financing; or

- the financial institution has doubts about the veracity or adequacy of previously obtained customer identification data.

The customer due diligence (CDD) measures to be taken are as follows:

a) Identifying the customer and verifying that customer's identity using reliable, independent source documents, data or information[35].

b) Identifying the beneficial owner, and taking reasonable measures to verify the identity of the beneficial owner such that the financial institution is satisfied that it knows who the beneficial owner is. For legal persons and arrangements this should include financial institutions taking

---

[35] Reliable, independent source documents, data or information will hereafter be referred to as "identification data".

reasonable measures to understand the ownership and control structure of the customer.

c) Obtaining information on the purpose and intended nature of the business relationship.

d) Conducting ongoing due diligence on the business relationship and scrutiny of transactions undertaken throughout the course of that relationship to ensure that the transactions being conducted are consistent with the institution's knowledge of the customer, their business and risk profile, including, where necessary, the source of funds.

Financial institutions should apply each of the CDD measures under *a)* to *d)* above, but may determine the extent of such measures on a risk sensitive basis depending on the type of customer, business relationship or transaction. The measures that are taken should be consistent with any guidelines issued by competent authorities. For higher risk categories, financial institutions should perform enhanced due diligence. In certain circumstances, where there are low risks, countries may decide that financial institutions can apply reduced or simplified measures.

Financial institutions should verify the identity of the customer and beneficial owner before or during the course of establishing a business relationship or conducting transactions for occasional customers. Countries may permit financial institutions to complete the verification as soon as reasonably practicable following the establishment of the relationship, where the money laundering risks are effectively managed and where this is essential not to interrupt the normal conduct of business.

Where the financial institution is unable to comply with paragraphs *a)* to *c)* above, it should not open the account, commence business relations or perform the transaction; or should terminate the business relationship; and should consider making a suspicious transactions report in relation to the customer.

These requirements should apply to all new customers, though financial institutions should also apply this Recommendation to existing customers on the basis of materiality and risk, and should conduct due diligence on such existing relationships at appropriate times.

6.*   Financial institutions should, in relation to politically exposed persons, in addition to performing normal due diligence measures:

a) Have appropriate risk management systems to determine whether the customer is a politically exposed person.

b) Obtain senior management approval for establishing business relationships with such customers.

c) Take reasonable measures to establish the source of wealth and source of funds.

d) Conduct enhanced ongoing monitoring of the business relationship.

7.   Financial institutions should, in relation to cross-border correspondent banking and other similar relationships, in addition to performing normal due diligence measures:

a) Gather sufficient information about a respondent institution to understand fully the nature of the respondent's business and to determine from publicly available information the reputation of the institution and the quality of supervision, including whether it has been subject to a money laundering or terrorist financing investigation or regulatory action.

b) Assess the respondent institution's anti-money laundering and terrorist financing controls.

c) Obtain approval from senior management before establishing new correspondent relationships.

d) Document the respective responsibilities of each institution.

e) With respect to "payable-through accounts", be satisfied that the respondent bank has verified the identity of and performed on-going due diligence on the customers having direct access to accounts of the correspondent and that it is able to provide relevant customer identification data upon request to the correspondent bank.

8.   Financial institutions should pay special attention to any money laundering threats that may arise from new or developing technologies that might favour anonymity, and take measures, if needed, to prevent

their use in money laundering schemes. In particular, financial institutions should have policies and procedures in place to address any specific risks associated with non-face to face business relationships or transactions.

9.* Countries may permit financial institutions to rely on intermediaries or other third parties to perform elements *a)-c)* of the CDD process or to introduce business, provided that the criteria set out below are met. Where such reliance is permitted, the ultimate responsibility for customer identification and verification remains with the financial institution relying on the third party.

The criteria that should be met are as follows:

a) A financial institution relying upon a third party should immediately obtain the necessary information concerning elements *a)-c)* of the CDD process. Financial institutions should take adequate steps to satisfy themselves that copies of identification data and other relevant documentation relating to the CDD requirements will be made available from the third party upon request without delay.

b) The financial institution should satisfy itself that the third party is regulated and supervised for, and has measures in place to comply with CDD requirements in line with Recommendations 5 and 10.

It is left to each country to determine in which countries the third party that meets the conditions can be based, having regard to information available on countries that do not or do not adequately apply the FATF Recommendations.

10.* Financial institutions should maintain, for at least five years, all necessary records on transactions, both domestic or international, to enable them to comply swiftly with information reconstruction of individual transactions (including the amounts and types of currency involved if any) so as to provide, if necessary, evidence for prosecution of criminal activity.

Financial institutions should keep records on the identification data obtained through the customer due diligence process (*e.g.* copies or records of official identification documents like passports, identity cards, driving licenses or similar documents), account files and business correspondence for at least five years after the business relationship is ended.

The identification data and transaction records should be available to domestic competent authorities upon appropriate authority.

11.*   Financial institutions should pay special attention to all complex, unusual large transactions, and all unusual patterns of transactions, which have no apparent economic or visible lawful purpose. The background and purpose of such transactions should, as far as possible, be examined, the findings established in writing, and be available to help competent authorities and auditors.

12.*   The customer due diligence and record-keeping requirements set out in Recommendations 5, 6, and 8 to 11 apply to designated non-financial businesses and professions in the following situations:

a) Casinos – when customers engage in financial transactions equal to or above the applicable designated threshold.

b) Real estate agents – when they are involved in transactions for their client concerning the buying and selling of real estate.

c) Dealers in precious metals and dealers in precious stones – when they engage in any cash transaction with a customer equal to or above the applicable designated threshold.

d) Lawyers, notaries, other independent legal professionals and accountants when they prepare for or carry out transactions for their client concerning the following activities:

- buying and selling of real estate;

- managing of client money, securities or other assets;

- management of bank, savings or securities accounts;

- organisation of contributions for the creation, operation or management of companies;

- creation, operation or management of legal persons or arrangements, and buying and selling of business entities.

e) Trust and company service providers when they prepare for or carry out transactions for a client concerning the activities listed in the definition in the Glossary.

Reporting of suspicious transactions and compliance

13.* If a financial institution suspects or has reasonable grounds to suspect that funds are the proceeds of a criminal activity, or are related to terrorist financing, it should be required, directly by law or regulation, to report promptly its suspicions to the financial intelligence unit (FIU).

14.* Financial institutions, their directors, officers and employees should be:

a) Protected by legal provisions from criminal and civil liability for breach of any restriction on disclosure of information imposed by contract or by any legislative, regulatory or administrative provision, if they report their suspicions in good faith to the FIU, even if they did not know precisely what the underlying criminal activity was, and regardless of whether illegal activity actually occurred.

b) Prohibited by law from disclosing the fact that a suspicious transaction report (STR) or related information is being reported to the FIU.

15.* Financial institutions should develop programmes against money laundering and terrorist financing. These programmes should include:

a) The development of internal policies, procedures and controls, including appropriate compliance management arrangements, and adequate screening procedures to ensure high standards when hiring employees.

b) An ongoing employee training programme.

c) An audit function to test the system.

16.* The requirements set out in Recommendations 13 to 15, and 21 apply to all designated non-financial businesses and professions, subject to the following qualifications:

a) Lawyers, notaries, other independent legal professionals and accountants should be required to report suspicious transactions when, on behalf of or for a client, they engage in a financial transaction in relation to the activities described in Recommendation 12*d)*. Countries are strongly encouraged to extend the reporting requirement to the rest of the professional activities of accountants, including auditing.

b) Dealers in precious metals and dealers in precious stones should be required to report suspicious transactions when they engage in any cash transaction with a customer equal to or above the applicable designated threshold.

c) Trust and company service providers should be required to report suspicious transactions for a client when, on behalf of or for a client, they engage in a transaction in relation to the activities referred to in Recommendation 12*e)*.

Lawyers, notaries, other independent legal professionals, and accountants acting as independent legal professionals, are not required to report their suspicions if the relevant information was obtained in circumstances where they are subject to professional secrecy or legal professional privilege.

Other measures to deter money laundering and terrorist financing

17. Countries should ensure that effective, proportionate and dissuasive sanctions, whether criminal, civil or administrative, are available to deal with natural or legal persons covered by these Recommendations that fail to comply with anti-money laundering or terrorist financing requirements.

18. Countries should not approve the establishment or accept the continued operation of shell banks. Financial institutions should refuse to enter into, or continue, a correspondent banking relationship with shell banks. Financial institutions should also guard against establishing relations with respondent foreign financial institutions that permit their accounts to be used by shell banks.

19.* Countries should consider:

a) Implementing feasible measures to detect or monitor the physical cross-border transportation of currency and bearer negotiable instruments, subject to strict safeguards to ensure proper use of information and without impeding in any way the freedom of capital movements.

b) The feasibility and utility of a system where banks and other financial institutions and intermediaries would report all domestic and international currency transactions above a fixed amount, to a national central agency with a computerised data base, available to competent authorities for use in money laundering or terrorist financing cases, subject to strict safeguards to ensure proper use of the information.

20. Countries should consider applying the FATF Recommendations to businesses and professions, other than designated non-financial businesses and professions, that pose a money laundering or terrorist financing risk.

Countries should further encourage the development of modern and secure techniques of money management that are less vulnerable to money laundering.

Measures to be taken with respect to countries that do not or insufficiently comply with the FATF Recommendations

21. Financial institutions should give special attention to business relationships and transactions with persons, including companies and financial institutions, from countries which do not or insufficiently apply the FATF Recommendations. Whenever these transactions have no apparent economic or visible lawful purpose, their background and purpose should, as far as possible, be examined, the findings established in writing, and be available to help competent authorities. Where such a country continues not to apply or insufficiently applies the FATF Recommendations, countries should be able to apply appropriate countermeasures.

22. Financial institutions should ensure that the principles applicable to financial institutions, which are mentioned above are also applied to branches and majority owned subsidiaries located abroad, especially in countries which do not or insufficiently apply the FATF Recommendations, to the extent that local applicable laws and regulations permit. When local applicable laws and regulations prohibit this implementation, competent authorities in the country of the parent

institution should be informed by the financial institutions that they cannot apply the FATF Recommendations.

Regulation and supervision

23.*   Countries should ensure that financial institutions are subject to adequate regulation and supervision and are effectively implementing the FATF Recommendations. Competent authorities should take the necessary legal or regulatory measures to prevent criminals or their associates from holding or being the beneficial owner of a significant or controlling interest or holding a management function in a financial institution.

For financial institutions subject to the Core Principles, the regulatory and supervisory measures that apply for prudential purposes and which are also relevant to money laundering, should apply in a similar manner for anti-money laundering and terrorist financing purposes.

Other financial institutions should be licensed or registered and appropriately regulated, and subject to supervision or oversight for anti-money laundering purposes, having regard to the requests from the competent authorities. Such records must be sufficient to permit risk of money laundering or terrorist financing in that sector. At a minimum, businesses providing a service of money or value transfer, or of money or currency changing should be licensed or registered, and subject to effective systems for monitoring and ensuring compliance with national requirements to combat money laundering and terrorist financing.

24.   Designated non-financial businesses and professions should be subject to regulatory and supervisory measures as set out below.

a) Casinos should be subject to a comprehensive regulatory and supervisory regime that ensures that they have effectively implemented the necessary anti-money laundering and terrorist-financing measures. At a minimum:

- casinos should be licensed;

- competent authorities should take the necessary legal or regulatory measures to prevent criminals or their associates from holding or being the beneficial owner of a significant or controlling interest, holding a management function in, or being an operator of a casino;

- competent authorities should ensure that casinos are effectively supervised for compliance with requirements to combat money laundering and terrorist financing.

b) Countries should ensure that the other categories of designated non-financial businesses and professions are subject to effective systems for monitoring and ensuring their compliance with requirements to combat money laundering and terrorist financing. This should be performed on a risk-sensitive basis. This may be performed by a government authority or by an appropriate self-regulatory organisation, provided that such an organisation can ensure that its members comply with their obligations to combat money laundering and terrorist financing.

25.* The competent authorities should establish guidelines, and provide feedback which will assist financial institutions and designated non-financial businesses and professions in applying national measures to combat money laundering and terrorist financing, and in particular, in detecting and reporting suspicious transactions.

C. INSTITUTIONAL AND OTHER MEASURES NECESSARY IN SYSTEMS FOR COMBATING MONEY LAUNDERING AND TERRORIST FINANCING

Competent authorities, their powers and resources

26.* Countries should establish a FIU that serves as a national centre for the receiving (and, as permitted, requesting), analysis and dissemination of STR and other information regarding potential money laundering or terrorist financing. The FIU should have access, directly or indirectly, on a timely basis to the financial, administrative and law enforcement information that it requires to properly undertake its functions, including the analysis of STR.

27.* Countries should ensure that designated law enforcement authorities have responsibility for money laundering and terrorist financing investigations. Countries are encouraged to support and develop, as far as possible, special investigative techniques suitable for the investigation of money laundering, such as controlled delivery, undercover operations and other relevant techniques. Countries are also encouraged to use other effective mechanisms such as the use of permanent or temporary groups specialised in asset investigation, and co-operative investigations with appropriate competent authorities in other countries.

28. When conducting investigations of money laundering and underlying predicate offences, competent authorities should be able to obtain documents and information for use in those investigations, and in prosecutions and related actions. This should include powers to use compulsory measures for the production of records held by financial institutions and other persons, for the search of persons and premises, and for the seizure and obtaining of evidence.

29. Supervisors should have adequate powers to monitor and ensure compliance by financial institutions with requirements to combat money laundering and terrorist financing, including the authority to conduct inspections. They should be authorised to compel production of any information from financial institutions that is relevant to monitoring such compliance, and to impose adequate administrative sanctions for failure to comply with such requirements.

30. Countries should provide their competent authorities involved in combating money laundering and terrorist financing with adequate financial, human and technical resources. Countries should have in place processes to ensure that the staff of those authorities are of high integrity.

31. Countries should ensure that policy makers, the FIU, law enforcement and supervisors have effective mechanisms in place which enable them to co-operate, and where appropriate co-ordinate domestically with each other concerning the development and implementation of policies and activities to combat money laundering and terrorist financing.

32. Countries should ensure that their competent authorities can review the effectiveness of their systems to combat money laundering and terrorist financing systems by maintaining comprehensive statistics on matters relevant to the effectiveness and efficiency of such systems. This

should include statistics on the STR received and disseminated; on money laundering and terrorist financing investigations, prosecutions and convictions; on property frozen, seized and confiscated; and on mutual legal assistance or other international requests for co-operation.

Transparency of legal persons and arrangements

33. Countries should take measures to prevent the unlawful use of legal persons by money launderers. Countries should ensure that there is adequate, accurate and timely information on the beneficial ownership and control of legal persons that can be obtained or accessed in a timely fashion by competent authorities. In particular, countries that have legal persons that are able to issue bearer shares should take appropriate measures to ensure that they are not misused for money laundering and be able to demonstrate the adequacy of those measures. Countries could consider measures to facilitate access to beneficial ownership and control information to financial institutions undertaking the requirements set out in Recommendation 5.

34. Countries should take measures to prevent the unlawful use of legal arrangements by money launderers. In particular, countries should ensure that there is adequate, accurate and timely information on express trusts, including information on the settlor, trustee and beneficiaries, that can be obtained or accessed in a timely fashion by competent authorities. Countries could consider measures to facilitate access to beneficial ownership and control information to financial institutions undertaking the requirements set out in Recommendation 5.

D. INTERNATIONAL CO-OPERATION

35. Countries should take immediate steps to become party to and implement fully the Vienna Convention, the Palermo Convention, and the 1999 United Nations International Convention for the Suppression of the Financing of Terrorism. Countries are also encouraged to ratify and implement other relevant international conventions, such as the 1990 Council of Europe Convention on Laundering, Search, Seizure and Confiscation of the Proceeds from Crime and the 2002 Inter-American Convention against Terrorism.

Mutual legal assistance and extradition

36.   Countries should rapidly, constructively and effectively provide the widest possible range of mutual legal assistance in relation to money laundering and terrorist financing investigations, prosecutions, and related proceedings. In particular, countries should:

a) Not prohibit or place unreasonable or unduly restrictive conditions on the provision of mutual legal assistance.

b) Ensure that they have clear and efficient processes for the execution of mutual legal assistance requests.

c) Not refuse to execute a request for mutual legal assistance on the sole ground that the offence is also considered to involve fiscal matters.

d) Not refuse to execute a request for mutual legal assistance on the grounds that laws require financial institutions to maintain secrecy or confidentiality.

Countries should ensure that the powers of their competent authorities required under Recommendation 28 are also available for use in response to requests for mutual legal assistance, and if consistent with their domestic framework, in response to direct requests from foreign judicial or law enforcement authorities to domestic counterparts.

To avoid conflicts of jurisdiction, consideration should be given to devising and applying mechanisms for determining the best venue for prosecution of defendants in the interests of justice in cases that are subject to prosecution in more than one country.

37.   Countries should, to the greatest extent possible, render mutual legal assistance notwithstanding the absence of dual criminality.

Where dual criminality is required for mutual legal assistance or extradition, that requirement should be deemed to be satisfied regardless of whether both countries place the offence within the same category of offence or denominate the offence by the same terminology, provided that both countries criminalise the conduct underlying the offence.

38.   There should be authority to take expeditious action in response to requests by foreign countries to identify, freeze, seize and confiscate

property laundered, proceeds from money laundering or predicate offences, instrumentalities used in or intended for use in the commission of these offences, or property of corresponding value. There should also be arrangements for co-ordinating seizure and confiscation proceedings, which may include the sharing of confiscated assets.

39. Countries should recognise money laundering as an extraditable offence. Each country should either extradite its own nationals, or where a country does not do so solely on the grounds of nationality, that country should, at the request of the country seeking extradition, submit the case without undue delay to its competent authorities for the purpose of prosecution of the offences set forth in the request. Those authorities should take their decision and conduct their proceedings in the same manner as in the case of any other offence of a serious nature under the domestic law of that country. The countries concerned should co-operate with each other, in particular on procedural and evidentiary aspects, to ensure the efficiency of such prosecutions.

Subject to their legal frameworks, countries may consider simplifying extradition by allowing direct transmission of extradition requests between appropriate ministries, extraditing persons based only on warrants of arrests or judgements, and/or introducing a simplified extradition of consenting persons who waive formal extradition proceedings.

Other forms of co-operation

40.* Countries should ensure that their competent authorities provide the widest possible range of international co-operation to their foreign counterparts. There should be clear and effective gateways to facilitate the prompt and constructive exchange directly between counterparts, either spontaneously or upon request, of information relating to both money laundering and the underlying predicate offences. Exchanges should be permitted without unduly restrictive conditions. In particular:

a) Competent authorities should not refuse a request for assistance on the sole ground that the request is also considered to involve fiscal matters.

b) Countries should not invoke laws that require financial institutions to maintain secrecy or confidentiality as a ground for refusing to provide co-operation.

c) Competent authorities should be able to conduct inquiries; and where possible, investigations; on behalf of foreign counterparts.

Where the ability to obtain information sought by a foreign competent authority is not within the mandate of its counterpart, countries are also encouraged to permit a prompt and constructive exchange of information with non-counterparts. Co-operation with foreign authorities other than counterparts could occur directly or indirectly. When uncertain about the appropriate avenue to follow, competent authorities should first contact their foreign counterparts for assistance.

Countries should establish controls and safeguards to ensure that information exchanged by competent authorities is used only in an authorised manner, consistent with their obligations concerning privacy and data protection.

GLOSSARY

In these Recommendations the following abbreviations and references are used:

Beneficial owner refers to the natural person(s) who ultimately owns or controls a customer and/or the person on whose behalf a transaction is being conducted. It also incorporates those persons who exercise ultimate effective control over a legal person or arrangement.

Core Principles refers to the Core Principles for Effective Banking Supervision issued by the Basel Committee on Banking Supervision, the Objectives and Principles for Securities Regulation issued by the International Organisation of Securities Commissions, and the Insurance Supervisory Principles issued by the International Association of Insurance Supervisors.

Designated categories of offences means:

- participation in an organised criminal group and racketeering;
- terrorism, including terrorist financing;
- trafficking in human beings and migrant smuggling;
- sexual exploitation, including sexual exploitation of children;
- illicit trafficking in narcotic drugs and psychotropic substances;
- illicit arms trafficking;
- illicit trafficking in stolen and other goods;
- corruption and bribery;
- fraud;
- counterfeiting currency;
- counterfeiting and piracy of products;
- environmental crime;
- murder, grievous bodily injury;
- kidnapping, illegal restraint and hostage-taking;
- robbery or theft;
- smuggling;
- extortion;
- forgery;
- piracy; and
- insider trading and market manipulation.

When deciding on the range of offences to be covered as predicate offences under each of the categories listed above, each country may decide, in accordance with its domestic law, how it will define those offences and the nature of any particular elements of those offences that make them serious offences.

Designated non-financial businesses and professions means:

a) Casinos (which also includes internet casinos).
b) Real estate agents.
c) Dealers in precious metals.
d) Dealers in precious stones.
e) Lawyers, notaries, other independent legal professionals and accountants – this refers to sole practitioners, partners or employed professionals within professional firms. It is not meant to refer to "internal" professionals that are employees of other types of businesses, nor to professionals working for government agencies, who may already be subject to measures that would combat money laundering.
f) Trust and Company Service Providers refers to all persons or businesses that are not covered elsewhere under these Recommendations, and which as a business, provide any of the following services to third parties:

- acting as a formation agent of legal persons;
- acting as (or arranging for another person to act as) a director or secretary of a company, a partner of a partnership, or a similar position in relation to other legal persons;
- providing a registered office; business address or accommodation, correspondence or administrative address for a company, a partnership or any other legal person or arrangement;
- acting as (or arranging for another person to act as) a trustee of an express trust;
- acting as (or arranging for another person to act as) a nominee shareholder for another person.

Designated threshold refers to the amount set out in the Interpretative Notes.

Financial institutions means any person or entity who conducts as a business one or more of the following activities or operations for or on behalf of a customer:

1. Acceptance of deposits and other repayable funds from the public.[36]

---

[36] This also captures private banking.

2. Lending.[37]
3. Financial leasing.[38]
4. The transfer of money or value.[39]
5. Issuing and managing means of payment (*e.g.* credit and debit cards, cheques, traveller's cheques, money orders and bankers' drafts, electronic money).
6. Financial guarantees and commitments.
7. Trading in:
    a) money market instruments (cheques, bills, CDs, derivatives, etc.);
    b) foreign exchange;
    c) exchange, interest rate and index instruments;
    d) transferable securities;
    e) commodity futures trading.
8. Participation in securities issues and the provision of financial services related to such issues.
9. Individual and collective portfolio management.
10. Safekeeping and administration of cash or liquid securities on behalf of other persons.
11. Otherwise investing, administering or managing funds or money on behalf of other persons.
12. Underwriting and placement of life insurance and other investment related insurance.[40]
13. Money and currency changing.

---

[37] This includes inter alia: consumer credit; mortgage credit; factoring, with or without recourse; and finance of commercial transactions (including forfaiting).

[38] This does not extend to financial leasing arrangements in relation to consumer products.

[39] This applies to financial activity in both the formal or informal sector *e.g.* alternative remittance activity. See the Interpretative Note to Special Recommendation VI. It does not apply to any natural or legal person that provides financial institutions solely with message or other support systems for transmitting funds. See the Interpretative Note to Special Recommendation VII.

[40] This applies both to insurance undertakings and to insurance intermediaries (agents and brokers).

When a financial activity is carried out by a person or entity on an occasional or very limited basis (having regard to quantitative and absolute criteria) such that there is little risk of money laundering activity occurring, a country may decide that the application of anti-money laundering measures is not necessary, either fully or partially.

In strictly limited and justified circumstances, and based on a proven low risk of money laundering, a country may decide not to apply some or all of the Forty Recommendations to some of the financial activities stated above.

FIU means financial intelligence unit.

Legal arrangements refers to express trusts or other similar legal arrangements.

Legal persons refers to bodies corporate, foundations, anstalt, partnerships, or associations, or any similar bodies that can establish a permanent customer relationship with a financial institution or otherwise own property.

Payable-through accounts refers to correspondent accounts that are used directly by third parties to transact business on their own behalf.

Politically Exposed Persons (PEPs) are individuals who are or have been entrusted with prominent public functions in a foreign country, for example Heads of State or of government, senior politicians, senior government, judicial or military officials, senior executives of state owned corporations, important political party officials. Business relationships with family members or close associates of PEPs involve reputational risks similar to those with PEPs themselves. The definition is not intended to cover middle ranking or more junior individuals in the foregoing categories.

Shell bank means a bank incorporated in a jurisdiction in which it has no physical presence and which is unaffiliated with a regulated financial group.

STR refers to suspicious transaction reports.

Supervisors refers to the designated competent authorities responsible for ensuring compliance by financial institutions with requirements to combat money laundering and terrorist financing.

the FATF Recommendations refers to these Recommendations and to the FATF Special Recommendations on Terrorist Financing.

Interpretative Notes To The Forty Recommendations

General

1. Reference in this document to "countries" should be taken to apply equally to "territories" or "jurisdictions".

2. Recommendations 5-16 and 21-22 state that financial institutions or designated non-financial businesses and professions should take certain actions. These references require countries to take measures that will oblige financial institutions or designated non-financial businesses and professions to comply with each Recommendation. The basic obligations under Recommendations 5, 10 and 13 should be set out in law or regulation, while more detailed elements in those Recommendations, as well as obligations under other Recommendations, could be required either by law or regulation or by other enforceable means issued by a competent authority.

3. Where reference is made to a financial institution being satisfied as to a matter, that institution must be able to justify its assessment to competent authorities.

4. To comply with Recommendations 12 and 16, countries do not need to issue laws or regulations that relate exclusively to lawyers, notaries, accountants and the other designated non-financial businesses and professions so long as these businesses or professions are included in laws or regulations covering the underlying activities.

5. The Interpretative Notes that apply to financial institutions are also relevant to designated non-financial businesses and professions, where applicable.

Recommendations 5, 12 and 16

The designated thresholds for transactions (under Recommendations 5 and 12) are as follows:

- Financial institutions (for occasional customers under Recommendation 5) – USD/EUR 15 000.

- Casinos, including internet casinos (under Recommendation 12) – USD/EUR 3 000

- For dealers in precious metals and dealers in precious stones when engaged in any cash transaction (under Recommendations 12 and 16) – USD/EUR 15 000.

Financial transactions above a designated threshold include situations where the transaction is carried out in a single operation or in several operations that appear to be linked.

Recommendation 5

Customer due diligence and tipping off

1. If, during the establishment or course of the customer relationship, or when conducting occasional transactions, a financial institution suspects that transactions relate to money laundering or terrorist financing, then the institution should:

> *a)* Normally seek to identify and verify the identity of the customer and the beneficial owner, whether permanent or occasional, and irrespective of any exemption or any designated threshold that might otherwise apply.
>
> *b)* Make a STR to the FIU in accordance with Recommendation 13.

2. Recommendation 14 prohibits financial institutions, their directors, officers and employees from disclosing the fact that an STR or related information is being reported to the FIU. A risk exists that customers could be unintentionally tipped off when the financial institution is seeking to perform its customer due diligence (CDD) obligations in these circumstances. The customer's awareness of a possible STR or investigation could compromise future efforts to investigate the suspected money laundering or terrorist financing operation.

3. Therefore, if financial institutions form a suspicion that transactions relate to money laundering or terrorist financing, they should take into account the risk of tipping off when performing the customer due diligence process. If the institution reasonably believes that performing the CDD process will tip-off the customer or potential customer, it may choose not to pursue that process, and should file an STR. Institutions should ensure that their employees are aware of and sensitive to these issues when conducting CDD.

CDD for legal persons and arrangements

4. When performing elements *a)* and *b)* of the CDD process in relation to legal persons or arrangements, financial institutions should:

> *a)* Verify that any person purporting to act on behalf of the customer is so authorised, and identify that person.

b) Identify the customer and verify its identity - the types of measures that would be normally needed to satisfactorily perform this function would require obtaining proof of incorporation or similar evidence of the legal status of the legal person or arrangement, as well as information concerning the customer's name, the names of trustees, legal form, address, directors, and provisions regulating the power to bind the legal person or arrangement.

c) Identify the beneficial owners, including forming an understanding of the ownership and control structure, and take reasonable measures to verify the identity of such persons. The types of measures that would be normally needed to satisfactorily perform this function would require identifying the natural persons with a controlling interest and identifying the natural persons who comprise the mind and management of the legal person or arrangement. Where the customer or the owner of the controlling interest is a public company that is subject to regulatory disclosure requirements, it is not necessary to seek to identify and verify the identity of any shareholder of that company.

The relevant information or data may be obtained from a public register, from the customer or from other reliable sources.

Reliance on identification and verification already performed

5. The CDD measures set out in Recommendation 5 do not imply that financial institutions have to repeatedly identify and verify the identity of each customer every time that a customer conducts a transaction. An institution is entitled to rely on the identification and verification steps that it has already undertaken unless it has doubts about the veracity of that information. Examples of situations that might lead an institution to have such doubts could be where there is a suspicion of money laundering in relation to that customer, or where there is a material change in the way that the customer's account is operated which is not consistent with the customer's business profile.

Timing of verification

6. Examples of the types of circumstances where it would be permissible for verification to be completed after the establishment of the business relationship, because it would be essential not to interrupt the normal conduct of business include:

- Non face-to-face business.
- Securities transactions. In the securities industry, companies and intermediaries may be required to perform transactions very rapidly,

according to the market conditions at the time the customer is contacting them, and the performance of the transaction may be required before verification of identity is completed.

- Life insurance business. In relation to life insurance business, countries may permit the identification and verification of the beneficiary under the policy to take place after having established the business relationship with the policyholder. However, in all such cases, identification and verification should occur at or before the time of payout or the time where the beneficiary intends to exercise vested rights under the policy.

7. Financial institutions will also need to adopt risk management procedures with respect to the conditions under which a customer may utilise the business relationship prior to verification. These procedures should include a set of measures such as a limitation of the number, types and/or amount of transactions that can be performed and the monitoring of large or complex transactions being carried out outside of expected norms for that type of relationship. Financial institutions should refer to the Basel CDD paper[41] (section 2.2.6.) for specific guidance on examples of risk management measures for non-face to face business.

Requirement to identify existing customers

8. The principles set out in the Basel CDD paper concerning the identification of existing customers should serve as guidance when applying customer due diligence processes to institutions engaged in banking activity, and could apply to other financial institutions where relevant.

Simplified or reduced CDD measures

9. The general rule is that customers must be subject to the full range of CDD measures, including the requirement to identify the beneficial owner. Nevertheless there are circumstances where the risk of money laundering or terrorist financing is lower, where information on the identity of the customer and the beneficial owner of a customer is publicly available, or where adequate checks and controls exist elsewhere in national systems. In such circumstances it could be reasonable for a country to allow its financial institutions to apply simplified or reduced CDD measures when identifying and verifying the identity of the customer and the beneficial owner.

---

[41] "Basel CDD paper" refers to the guidance paper on Customer Due Diligence for Banks issued by the Basel Committee on Banking Supervision in October 2001.

10. Examples of customers where simplified or reduced CDD measures could apply are:

- Financial institutions – where they are subject to requirements to combat money laundering and terrorist financing consistent with the FATF Recommendations and are supervised for compliance with those controls.
- Public companies that are subject to regulatory disclosure requirements.
- Government administrations or enterprises.

11. Simplified or reduced CDD measures could also apply to the beneficial owners of pooled accounts held by designated non financial businesses or professions provided that those businesses or professions are subject to requirements to combat money laundering and terrorist financing consistent with the FATF Recommendations and are subject to effective systems for monitoring and ensuring their compliance with those requirements. Banks should also refer to the Basel CDD paper (section 2.2.4.), which provides specific guidance concerning situations where an account holding institution may rely on a customer that is a professional financial intermediary to perform the customer due diligence on his or its own customers (*i.e.* the beneficial owners of the bank account). Where relevant, the CDD Paper could also provide guidance in relation to similar accounts held by other types of financial institutions.

12. Simplified CDD or reduced measures could also be acceptable for various types of products or transactions such as (examples only):

- Life insurance policies where the annual premium is no more than USD/€ 1 000 or a single premium of no more than USD/€ 2 500
- Insurance policies for pension schemes if there is no surrender clause and the policy cannot be used as collateral.
- A pension, superannuation or similar scheme that provides retirement benefits to employees, where contributions are made by way of deduction from wages and the scheme rules do not permit the assignment of a member's interest under the scheme.

13. Countries could also decide whether financial institutions could apply these simplified measures only to customers in its own jurisdiction or allow them to do for customers from any other jurisdiction that the original country is satisfied is in compliance with and has effectively implemented the FATF Recommendations.

Simplified CDD measures are not acceptable whenever there is suspicion of money laundering or terrorist financing or specific higher risk scenarios apply.

Recommendation 6

Countries are encouraged to extend the requirements of Recommendation 6 to individuals who hold prominent public functions in their own country.

Recommendation 9

This Recommendation does not apply to outsourcing or agency relationships.

This Recommendation also does not apply to relationships, accounts or transactions between financial institutions for their clients. Those relationships are addressed by Recommendations 5 and 7.

Recommendations 10 and 11

In relation to insurance business, the word "transactions" should be understood to refer to the insurance product itself, the premium payment and the benefits.

Recommendation 13

1. The reference to criminal activity in Recommendation 13 refers to:

   a) all criminal acts that would constitute a predicate offence for money laundering in the jurisdiction; or

   b) at a minimum to those offences that would constitute a predicate offence as required by Recommendation 1.

Countries are strongly encouraged to adopt alternative *a)*. All suspicious transactions, including attempted transactions, should be reported regardless of the amount of the transaction.

2. In implementing Recommendation 13, suspicious transactions should be reported by financial institutions regardless of whether they are also thought to involve tax matters. Countries should take into account that, in order to deter financial institutions from reporting a suspicious transaction, money launderers may seek to state *inter alia* that their transactions relate to tax matters.

Recommendation 14 (tipping off)

Where lawyers, notaries, other independent legal professionals and accountants acting as independent legal professionals seek to dissuade a client from engaging in illegal activity, this does not amount to tipping off.

Recommendation 15

The type and extent of measures to be taken for each of the requirements set out in the Recommendation should be appropriate having regard to the risk of money laundering and terrorist financing and the size of the business.

For financial institutions, compliance management arrangements should include the appointment of a compliance officer at the management level.

Recommendation 16

1. It is for each jurisdiction to determine the matters that would fall under legal professional privilege or professional secrecy. This would normally cover information lawyers, notaries or other independent legal professionals receive from or obtain through one of their clients: *a)* in the course of ascertaining the legal position of their client, or *b)* in performing their task of defending or representing that client in, or concerning judicial, administrative, arbitration or mediation proceedings. Where accountants are subject to the same obligations of secrecy or privilege, then they are also not required to report suspicious transactions.

2. Countries may allow lawyers, notaries, other independent legal professionals and accountants to send their STR to their appropriate self-regulatory organisations, provided that there are appropriate forms of co-operation between these organisations and the FIU.

Recommendation 19

1. To facilitate detection and monitoring of cash transactions, without impeding in any way the freedom of capital movements, countries could consider the feasibility of subjecting all cross-border transfers, above a given threshold, to verification, administrative monitoring, declaration or record keeping requirements.

2. If a country discovers an unusual international shipment of currency, monetary instruments, precious metals, or gems, etc., it should consider notifying, as appropriate, the Customs Service or other competent authorities of the countries from which the shipment originated and/or to which it is destined, and should co-operate with a view toward establishing the source, destination, and purpose of such shipment and toward the taking of appropriate action.

Recommendation 23

Recommendation 23 should not be read as to require the introduction of a system of regular review of licensing of controlling interests in financial institutions merely for anti-money laundering purposes, but as to stress the desirability of suitability review for controlling shareholders in financial institutions (banks and non-banks in particular) from a FATF point of view. Hence, where shareholder suitability (or "fit and proper") tests exist, the attention of supervisors should be drawn to their relevance for anti-money laundering purposes.

Recommendation 25

When considering the feedback that should be provided, countries should have regard to the FATF Best Practice Guidelines on Providing Feedback to Reporting Financial Institutions and Other Persons.

Recommendation 26

Where a country has created an FIU, it should consider applying for membership in the Egmont Group. Countries should have regard to the Egmont Group Statement of Purpose, and its Principles for Information Exchange Between Financial Intelligence Units for Money Laundering Cases. These documents set out important guidance concerning the role and functions of FIUs, and the mechanisms for exchanging information between FIU.

Recommendation 27

Countries should consider taking measures, including legislative ones, at the national level, to allow their competent authorities investigating money laundering cases to postpone or waive the arrest of suspected persons and/or the seizure of the money for the purpose of identifying persons involved in such activities or for evidence gathering. Without such measures the use of procedures such as controlled deliveries and undercover operations are precluded.

Recommendation 38

Countries should consider:

a) Establishing an asset forfeiture fund in its respective country into which all or a portion of confiscated property will be deposited for law enforcement, health, education, or other appropriate purposes.

b) Taking such measures as may be necessary to enable it to share among or between other countries confiscated property, in particular, when confiscation is directly or indirectly a result of co-ordinated law enforcement actions.

Recommendation 40

1. For the purposes of this Recommendation:

- "Counterparts" refers to authorities that exercise similar responsibilities and functions.

- "Competent authority" refers to all administrative and law enforcement authorities concerned with combating money laundering and terrorist financing, including the FIU and supervisors.

2. Depending on the type of competent authority involved and the nature and purpose of the co-operation, different channels can be appropriate for the exchange of information. Examples of mechanisms or channels that are used to exchange information include: bilateral or multilateral agreements or arrangements, memoranda of understanding, exchanges on the basis of reciprocity, or through appropriate international or regional organisations. However, this Recommendation is not intended to cover co-operation in relation to mutual legal assistance or extradition.

3. The reference to indirect exchange of information with foreign authorities other than counterparts covers the situation where the requested information passes from the foreign authority through one or more domestic or foreign authorities before being received by the requesting authority. The competent authority that requests the information should always make it clear for what purpose and on whose behalf the request is made.

4. FIUs should be able to make inquiries on behalf of foreign counterparts where this could be relevant to an analysis of financial transactions. At a minimum, inquiries should include:

- Searching its own databases, which would include information related to suspicious transaction reports.

- Searching other databases to which it may have direct or indirect access, including law enforcement databases, public databases, administrative databases and commercially available databases.

Where permitted to do so, FIUs should also contact other competent authorities and financial institutions in order to obtain relevant information.

ANNEX

Respondents to the FATF Self-Assessment Exercise for the Eight Special Recommendations on Terrorist Financing

FATF SELF ASSESSMENT EXERCISE FOR THE EIGHT SPECIAL RECOMMENDATIONS ON TERRORIST FINANCING

Responses from Jurisdictions as of 28 August 2003

This list contains the names of the countries or territories that have provided responses to the FATF Self Assessment Exercise, along with the date of their submission. For information on the FATF Self Assessment Exercise, please consult the following web address: *http://www.fatf-gafi.org/SAQTF_en.htm*.

Country/Territory:	Date	Country/Territory:	Date
Albania	02.08.2002	Andorra	03.07.2002
Anguilla	31.12.2001	Antigua and Barbuda	25.04.2002
Argentina	20.05.2002	Armenia	05.09.2002
Aruba	04.01.2002	Australia	22.03.2003
Austria	03.01.2002	Azerbaijan	23.10.2002
Bahamas	07.05.2002	Bahrain	08.01.2002
Barbados	31.12.2001	Belarus	10.09.2002
Belgium	08.01.2002	Belize	10.05.2002
Bermuda	01.05.2002	Brazil	15.03.2001
British Virgin Islands	07.10.2002	Bulgaria	04.09.2002
Canada	21.03.2002	Cayman Islands	02.05.2002
Chile	12.07.2002	China	13.09.2002
Colombia	03.06.2002	Cook Islands	02.09.2002
Costa Rica	03.05.2002	Croatia	02.07.2002
Cyprus	11.11.2002	Czech Republic	04.09.2002
Denmark	17.01.2002	Dominica	07.10.2002
Dominican Republic	01.05.2002	Egypt	06.06.2002
El Salvador	26.09.2002	Estonia	05.08.2002
Ethiopia	08.05.2002	Ecuador	20.01.2003
Finland	21.02.2002	Fiji	29.03.2003
FYR Macedonia	02.12.2002	France	22.04.2002
Germany	14.03.2002	Gibraltar	01.05.2002
Greece	25.01.2002	Grenada	02.08.2002
Guatemala	01.02.2002	Guernsey	01.05.2002

Country/Territory:	Date	Country/Territory:	Date
Haiti	02.10.2002	Hong Kong, China	19.10.2002
Hungary	26.04.2002	Iceland	11.01.2002
India	24.09.2002	Indonesia	14.06.2002
Ireland	09.01.2002	Isle of Man	16.04.2002
Israel	01.05.2002	Italy	09.01.2002
Jamaica	02.10.2002	Japan	13.06.2002
Jersey	30.04.2002	Korea, South	07.05.2002
Kuwait	01.09.2002	Kazakhstan	06.01.2003
Kyrgyzstan	28.09.2002	Labuan	04.01.2002
Latvia	08.07.2002	Lebanon	30.04.2002
Liechtenstein	23.04.2002	Lithuania	05.07.2002
Luxembourg	17.01.2002	Macau, China	29.04.2002
Malaysia	30.04.2002	Malta	02.07.2002
Mauritius	26.04.2002	Mexico	04.01.2002
Monaco	01.02.2002	Mongolia	02.05.2002
Montserrat	03.05.2002	Singapore	11.01.2002
Namibia	26.11.2002	Nauru	01.05.2002
Neth. Antilles	03.01.2002	Netherlands	04.01.2002
New Zealand	08.01.2002	Nicaragua	03.09.2002
Nigeria	02.05.2002	Norway	04.01.2002
Niue	25.11.2003	Oman	29.04.2002
Palau	22.07.2002	Panama	01.05.2002
Philippines	30.04.2002	Poland	10.03.2003
Portugal	28.03.2003	Qatar	29.12.2001
Romania	01.02.2002	Russia	08.10.2002
Saint Kitts and Nevis	02.05.2002	Saint Lucia	02.07.2002
St. Vincent and Grenadines	01.05.2002	Samoa	04.05.2002
San Marino	16.09.2002	Saudi Arabia	07.04.2003
Senegal	03.06.2002	Seychelles	02.05.2002
Slovakia	07.05.2002	Slovenia	06.02.2003
South Africa	11.06.2002	Spain	18.01.2002
Sri Lanka	01.08.2003	Sweden	11.06.2002
Switzerland	10.01.2002	Taiwan	02.05.2002
Tajikistan	13/02/2003	Thailand	26.08.2002
Trinidad and Tobago	20.09.2002	Turks and Caicos Islands	23.09.2002
Turkey	04.01.2002	Tuvalu	28.04.2002
Uganda	23.05.2002	Ukraine	30.04.2002
United Arab Emirates	23.09.2002	United Kingdom	04.01.2002
United States	21.01.2002	Uruguay	03.06.2002

Country/Territory:	Date	Country/Territory:	Date
Uzbekistan	30.08.2002	Vanuatu	15.06.2002
Venezuela	10.10.2002	Serbia/Montenegro: Serbia	10.09.2002
Serbia/Montenegro: Montenegro	06.09.2002	Serbia/Montenegro: Kosovo	10.06.2002

SUMMARY

	Received	Percentage
TOTAL RESPONSES (213 possible)	132	62%
FATF (29 members)	29	100%
European Commission (15 members)	15	100%
GCC (6 members)	6	100%
APG (26 members)	21	7%
CFATF (29 members)	26	90%
ESAAMLG (14 members)	5	36%
GAFISUD (9 members)	6	56%
MONEYVAL* (24 members)	22	92%
OGBS (19 members)	19	100%
OTHER (76 jurisdictions)	20	26%

* Council of Europe Select Committee of Experts on the Evaluation of Anti-Money Laundering Measures, formerly known as "PC-R-EV".

PRINTED IN FRANCE

(29 2004 01 1 P) – No. 53419